MODERN JET FIGHTERS

Motorbooks International
Publishers & Wholesalers Inc
Osceola, Wisconsin 54020, USA ®

MODERN JET FIGHTERS

First published in 1989 by Motorbooks International Publishers & Wholesalers, Inc.
P.O. Box 2, 729 Prospect Avenue, Osceola, Wisconsin 54020 USA

© International Defense Images   Printed and bound in Singapore

Motorbooks International is a certified trademark registered with the United States Patent Office

The information in this book is true and complete to the best of our knowledge. All recommendations are made
without any guarantee on the part of the authors or publisher, who also disclaim any liability incurred
in connection with the use of this data or specific details.

Library of Congress Cataloging-in-Publication Data

ISBN 0-87938-353-4

Motorbooks International books are also available at discounts in bulk quantity for industrial
or sales promotional use. For details write to Special Sales Manager at the Publisher's Address.

CONTENTS

4   **Profile: Serge Dassault**
by J. Philip Geddes

9   **Foreign Fighters**
A pictorial review

14   **Stealth**
by Nick Nichols

17   **Hawk**
by Terry Treadwell

23   **Pampa**
by Terry Treadwell

26   **MiG-29**
by William Sweetman

33   **TAC**
by Joe Poyer

44   **Eurofighter**
by Malcolm Lowe

49   **Rafale Radar**

50   **Matra Missile**

51   **AMRAAM**
by J. Philip Geddes

55   **F-16**
by Damian Housman

65   **Israeli Air Force**
by Lon Nordeen

74   **ATF/ATA**
by Erik Simonsen

82   **Spaceplane**
by John Guthrie

88   **Americas' Best**
Top U.S. Fighters

EDITORIAL STAFF

Mi Seitelman
Gary L. Kieffer
Philip Farris
Susan Turner

Design by
David Polewski

PHOTOGRAPHY/ILLUSTRATIONS

Mi Seitelman: pgs. 1 thru 3, 30 top left & center, 30 & 31 center-right, 58 bottom & center, 90 & 91, 94 thru 96
Frederick Sutter: Cover 1 , pgs. 23 thru 29, 30 lower left, 31 upper right, 32 thru 39, 42 & 43
Gary L. Kieffer: pg. 30 middle-center
John Batchelor: pgs.54-55
Jeffery Ethell: pgs. 10 & 11, 30 ctr. left, 40 & 41, 56 & 57
Anna Clopet: pgs. 5 thru 8
Michael Anselmo: pg. 58 top
Ken Kotik: pgs. 66, 69 upper right
Stan Jones: pgs. 76, 78
Erik Simonsen: pg. 79 bottom
Joe Cupido: pg. 31 upper left, 92 & 93
Steve Rice : pg. 86 lower left
Darryl Heikes: pgs. 80 & 81
Ken Hackman / USAF: pg. 16
Alain Ernoult / AMD - BA / Aviaplans: pg. 47
Robert Genat: pgs. 88 & 89
Herman Potgieter: pgs. 9, 12 & 13

Photo research provided by:
Jonathan Scott Arms and Sheri Marshall, IDI

Sandia National Laboratories: pgs. 82 & 83
McDonnell-Douglas: pgs. 20, 22 bottom, 79 top
Pilatus: pg. 21 top
General Dynamics: pgs. 51, 60, 87 top
Hughes Aircraft: pgs. 61 thru 63
Raytheon: pg. 64
NASA Langley Research Center: pgs. 84 & 85 top center
Messerschmitt-Bolkow-Blohm: pg. 85 bottom
Martin Marietta: pg. 86
Rockwell International: pg. 87 bottom
Thomson-CSF: pg. 49
British Aerospace: pgs.17 thru 19, 21 bottom, 22 top, 48
AMD-BA/Aviaplans: pg. 46
Lockheed: pgs.74 &75
Israel Air Force: pgs. 65, 67 thru 69, 70 thru 73
U.S. Air Force: pgs. 15, 53, 59 upper right, 77

PROFILE: Serge Dassault

President & CEO of Avions Marcel Dassault-Breguet Aviation
A French Point of View

by J. Philip Geddes

France has always had a consuming passion for aviation. Manned flight began there and has been nurtured ever since. It is no coincidence that aeronautical history is replete with great French names and their achievements. This passion for things that fly, which continues unabated to this day, supports a very high level of technology and a broad production base. That France would want to devote so much of its resources to aeronautics is something of a mystery to many Americans, who in dominating the world of aerospace, would like to rationalize design and production in other parts of the world around U.S. products, often in the name of a common defense, usually citing the logic of cost efficiency. The French don't care. As Mr. Dassault explains, France has every intention of retaining every facet of its capacity to design and build aircraft from the wheels up and is willing to pay the price. Dassault-Breguet has produced very large numbers of Mirage fighters for France and many countries scattered around the world; in fact, up to two thirds of production is exported. Dassault has also been very successful with its Mystere Falcon line of business jets. The Breguet part of the company retains a position in maritime patrol with the Atlantique 2. Dassault-Breguet's latest creation, the high performance Rafale, is a fighter for the world, Mr. Dassault says, not just France.

Over the last couple of years, there has been dissension in Europe over cooperation on a next generation European Fighter Aircraft (EFA) and complaints in France about the cost of Rafale. But France, once again, has decided to go it alone. France turned its back on the next generation fighter using the very cold logic of Mr. Dassault expressed in this interview -- it is simply not in the country's best interests; the Eurofighter does not fit the requirement; that is, the French Air Force's view of the requirement. Funds for Rafale have been increased in the 1989 defense budget estimates, with support from the Mitterand Government, ending the arguments on going ahead. Estimates for a 336-plane program (250 for the Air Force and 86 for the Navy) run to 40 billion French francs (Ffr) for

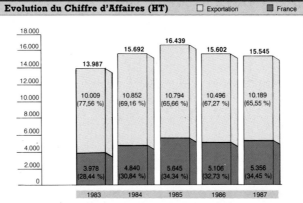

Evolution du Chiffre d'Affaires (HT)   ☐ Exportation   ■ France

development, and Ffr 80 billion for production. Dassault figures it will cost Ffr 80 billion to develop EFA

The present company was formed as the result of Avions Marcel Dassault and Breguet Aviation merging in 1971. Marcel Dassault, the founder, whose name still graces the company was a tough, passionate, national force in politics and industry who died in 1984. Marcel Dassault was a household word, embodying in a sense the pride of the people in his success and predictable outrage at anything that annoyed him. To pilots he was fighters. For example, a generation of pilots for good luck, when kicking in the afterburner at takeoff, would say "Chauffes Marcel" (turn on the heat

Marcel). The machines themselves were sound, high-performance, responsive, and made in France. In 1979, 20 percent of the company's stock was assigned to the French government and this amount was raised to 46 percent in 1979 with some shares holding double voting rights, making the state a majority shareholder.

Serge Dassault runs Dassault-Breguet without the theatrics of his father, a tough act to follow perhaps, but the company while not without problems is doing well. Turnover, that is deliveries, for the years 1983 through 1987, are shown in the chart at left. The ability of the company to export is vividly portrayed, rising to 66 percent in 1987, with the 34 percent going to the French government. Roughly one third of total export in 1987 was dedicated to civil sales of the company's broad line of Mystere Falcon business jets, the most recent of which is the Falcon 900. Even with the civil element removed, military exports in 1987 roughly equal sales to the French government. In the four previous years charted, however, military exports are close to double the volume of French government business which has concentrated attention outside the company on what comes next. To Serge Dassault, the answer is very simple - Rafale. Exports may decline temporarily, but build the right machine, he says, and the future will take care of itself.

Profitability declined from Ffr 293.4 million in 1986 to Ffr 191.6 million in 1987 (at current exchange rates, there are approximately six francs to a dollar). Mr. Dassault told his stockholders earlier this year that he saw 1987

as a year of transition and a new beginning based on orders at the end of that year rising to Ffr 13.4 billion (with 85 aircraft ordered) from Ffr 8.8 billion the year before. Within the company there has been a huge effort to cut costs and modernize facilities. Studies focussed on a maximum effort to export the Mirage 2000, with different versions to match needs, and continued investment in the civil Falcon. 1988 marked the beginning of development of the production Rafale (Model-D), for the Air Force, and the carrier-borne M-model for the Navy. New cooperation with foreign governments on "future" combat aircraft is being stressed by the company.

While 1987 was not a favorable year for export aircraft orders, 1988 was expected to pick up with new orders from South America for the Mirage III, and good prospects in the Middle East and Asia for the Mirage 2000 fighter, Alpha Jet trainer and the Atlantique 2 sea patrol aircraft. The Mirage 2000 is currently being built at the rate of 60 a year, which will hold until the Rafale production begins in 1996. Egypt, India, Peru, Abu Dhabi, Greece and Jordan are already customers for the Mirage 2000. Dassault lost competitions to provide the the Mirage 2000 to Kuwait and Switzerland. Space activities are primarily concerned with the CNES Hermes manned, reentry-research vehicle.

Dassault-Breguet employs approximately 14,000 people in 13 different plants scattered around the country: four are close to Paris Including St. Cloud, the principal design office and where military prototypes are created. It can be assumed that the widespread physical plants are a very useful factor in terms of political influence. As in any aircraft industry, the infrastructure supporting the largest Dassault plants is huge, producing as many hours of work outside the company as there are inside.

Mr. Serge Dassault entered Generale Aeronautique Marcel Dassault in 1951 and became head of flight test. Before becoming general manager of Electronique

Marcel Dassault, a subsidiary company, he directed exports. In addition to being the CEO of Avions Marcel Dassault-Breguet, Mr. Dassault is also the CEO of what is now Electronique "Serge" Dassault. Mr. Dassault has headed the organization of the Salon Aeronautique or Paris Air Show for a number of years, under the auspices of GIFAS -- the Groupement des Industries Francaises Aeronautiques et Spatiales.

The following comments by Mr. Dassault are from a recent interview in Paris with IDI, translated and edited from French:

International cooperation

I believe that cooperation is necessary for countries that do not have the technological capacity to develop a weapon system such as a fighter plane, helicopter and so on, on their own. For example, cooperation is indispensable for countries like Belgium, Italy, and Spain, even Germany, since they do not all have the industrial means to develop the airframe, the powerplant, the radars, and the missiles alone. This is not the case with France. France has the technical means and competence to build all of the systems for an aircraft. This capability is an advantage. France can thus keep its autonomy and fit its production to its proper needs.

And the other side of a cooperative program is that when you pay less you also make less.

The British, for example, are capable of developing missiles, powerplants and all the systems,. They have chosen a European common development, as in the Tornado and EFA, as the right thing to do. But Britain keeps full leadership for the engines and most of the airframe. Now when Britain sells a Tornado, she sells 30% of the aircraft, because she builds only 30%; the remainder is built by Italy and Germany. When we in France sell a Rafale, we sell 100% so that we have more interest in selling overseas than Britain has.

I believe that in the European objectives for the post-1992 period, defense issues are not a concern. Each country remains the master of its own defense. In my opinion, I do not think things will change much, not in any case for a long time. All this does not prevent Dassault from cooperating on a few programs such as Atlantique and Apha Jet. Other programs are under study with European and even non-European countries. Anyway, the French government makes such decisions, not Dassault.

Funding Rafale

Any defense program costs a lot, whether it is a plane, a helicopter, an aircraft carrier, a tank, or missile -- everything is expensive. The problem is one of determining if a country should go it alone on a program that it considers indispensable for its defense. Against this background, Rafale is not more expensive than any other program.

Whether there is to be enough money for developing aircraft, missiles, an aircraft-carrier, or helicopters alone or with other countries, is a government decision. It's the same in the United States. If the government decides to build an aircraft, it will find the money. Some programs in the U.S. cost much much more than in France. Compare the cost of programs such as the ATA and B-2 aircraft. They will cost America four or five times more than what we will spend. Eurofighter development will cost double the Rafale program, at

Ffr 80 billion minimum. Rafale then, is not as expensive as all that. In fact, Rafale is not much more expensive than the Mirage 2000 program and when we built the Mirage 2000 nobody raised their voice. For the Rafale program, we will spend 2% of the annual defense budget per year, which is not something extraordinary. The defense budget in France is 200 billion francs a year and we will spend 4 billion each year (for development) for 10 years. That makes 2%.

Countering criticism

The criticism of Rafale comes from journalists at l'Express, who have found a way to sell their newspaper by making great declarations that are wrong. In truth everything that l'Express said was false. The report they mention, a secret government report, is on the contrary a good report for Rafale. So all that L'Express said was false and could even be attacked legally. This affair is something invented by journalists but has nothing to do with reality. The newspaper's attack has changed nothing, either way. The program is firm. The Eurofighter did not suit the French Air Forces so they started their own program. That program is Rafale. The prototype will make its maiden flight in 1991 and production deliveries will start in 1996.

Exporting Rafale

We believe that a lot of Rafales will be exported. Exports are beneficial since they provide work to the overall industry, help our political presence overseas and benefit the balance of payments for France. The market for Rafale outside France is very large and important. We are planning a program of at least 20 years and will produce maybe over 1,000 planes.

There is an easy rule in France. The French army, like many countries, has 450 fighter planes. Well, those planes must be changed all the time. France, now and in the coming years, needs to replace the Mirage 3, then the Mirage F1, and then the Mirage 2000. A lot of other air forces will have to do likewise. Today, they are operating over 6,000 combat aircraft, all of which

will have to be replaced one day.

What is important is that the requirements of the French Air Force are very close to that of a great number of air forces worldwide, which need the same type of aircraft. They are not too big, not too expensive and are multi-purpose. All the aircraft that have been developed by us for the French Air Force are like that. In particular Rafale, for the first time in the world, is totally multi-purpose. It will thus fulfill a great many needs worldwide. While today air forces use interceptors, ground attack aircraft, tactical aircraft, in a word, all kinds of different aircraft, little by little all of these will be eliminated I believe in favor of the Rafale. An air force in the future will need only one aircraft, the Rafale.

The Eurofighter will be a heavier aircraft, with one mission, interception, and will come later I think than Rafale. It will, perhaps, fulfill other missions but will have, in my opinion, decidedly weaker prospects in an export market.

It is true that the British have important strength on the political level but whether they are more enterprising I don't know. We could have built an aircraft in common with the Germans but did not. It is easier for us to cooperate with the Germans than with the British, because we are more complementary to the Germans than the

British. Our problem in terms of exporting aircraft is the dollar.

U.S. content

There is no U.S. content in Rafale because if there were an American part, we could not export it. That's it. This American policy, which forbids or puts conditions on exporting American material, means for example, that even if we wanted to use American equipment, we could not. If we were to choose American equipment, we would have to submit to the conditions of the Congress who could refuse exports. We already have French regulations that control exports and it is unnecessary to add American ones. The French Government, for example, has decided not to sell armaments to South Africa so we are not allowed to sell there. That is a French decision, not an American one.

Buying American sea patrol

Europe can exist only if Europe buys its own material for defense. If Europe buys this from the U.S., it will stay dependenct on the U.S. There will be no European independence if Europe lacks leadership in the material for its own defense. So each time a European country buys from the U.S., it is a bad deal for Europe. When Europe has no equivalent then there is no choice. Take the AWACS (Boeing E-3A), there was nothing like that in Europe, so we bought AWACS from the U.S. But for Germany to buy sea patrol planes (LRAACA -- Lockheed's Long Range Air ASW Capable Aircraft, the P-3 replacement) from the U.S. would be an enormous error. Especially when the Germans have already participated in the Atlantique program and therefore it would be a step backward from Europe and become a great affair. One cannot pretend to be European when buying from the U.S.

We would be very happy to continue to sell to the United States but up to now there has not been much opportunity. We tried to sell the Alfa Jet (trainer) but the U.S. chose the Hawk. There is the Transport/Bomber Training Aircraft for training air crews and we believe that Falcon 100 is well suited for the program. And, why not, one day the U.S. might be interested in Rafale?

France is not closed to material that is U.S.-made. If, however, France makes the same equipment, then it is not worth it. We have made an agreement to study mounting AMRAAM (Hughes Aircraft's Advanced Medium Range Air-to-Air Missile) on Rafale because we believe that maybe some of our clients will want the missiles if they can get them.

Space

I think that space will grow but this activity must provide Dassault with profits. To be profitable for an industrial company, a product must be repetitive. Aircraft, missiles, and equipment become profitable because they are built in quantity. The problem with space is that there are only one or two units built and that's it. And there is unrestrained competition between several builders. From a company perspective, the point is not just to go into space, the point is to stay

profitable. We are working on Hermes, and have an important responsibility in the definition of the space ship. We are working with Aerospatiale and have several development and research programs for space.

Profitability and size

Size is not synonymous with efficiency. In the U.S. and in Europe right now there is a move to regroup aeronautical companies. In Germany and Britain it has already been done. People wonder why

France has not followed this route. There are small companies that have terrific success, then there are large ones with financial problems. There has been a regrouping in Germany around Airbus and MBB. MBB was having difficulties because of Airbus. Dornier too has had problems financing its 328 regional transports. But that does not apply to us. We prefer to be a company that may be smaller, not top heavy in management, but dynamic, well motivated, with solid employees who have a "team

spirit", rather than be a large group without the same motivation.

If I were at the head of a company of 80,000 people I would know nobody and could not be effective. So it is better to have medium companies dynamic, well structured and motivated than a typical enormous company with many divisions, where there is a president who is aware of nothing and it takes 15 days to make a decision.

Human and social relations have a great importance for us, and I spend a lot of time seeing the personnel and the directors, having meetings with all the employees of one factory. I recently gathered 6,000 employees at the Palais du Congres in Paris for two hours for a complete report on the company, including the validity of our plans, plus the technical, commercial and financial prospects.

Recently I was at our Toulouse, Biarritz, and Annecy factories, and will go soon to Bordeaux for a meeting with all the company and factory personnel. With everybody seated in a hangar, I speak about our problems and answer questions from the employees. I want the personnel to really understand the company's problems. Our industry has already been restructured. Twenty years ago there were five aircraft manufacturers. Today, there are only two left to share the work -- Aerospatiale and Dassault -- and we are no longer competitors but complementary. Part of the net profit of our whole company is given back to the employees after every balance-sheet is done. In this way, employees, who are always under the impression that they are not well enough paid, understand that profits are important. This participation in the benefits of profit-sharing, varies from year to year. Some years there are less benefits; but they must understand that when there is less profit, there is less money for them too. Instead of constantly asking for raises in their salaries and believing that the directors do not care, now they are conscious that the profitability of the enterprise is a fundamental element of the company and of their future. IDA

FOREIGN FIGHTERS

South African Air Force Mirage F1AZ

Chilean Air Force Mirage 50

South African Mirage F1AZ escorts defecting Mozambican MiG 17

STEALTH AIRCRAFT
They only come out at night!

by Nick Nichols

With due deference to the romantic image of the colorful aerobatics of sparring fighter pilots, it should be noted that the most successful aces have always been those who managed to spot their quarry first and, ideally, sanction him before he could even react. Efforts to capitalize on this philosophy through the development of less detectable hardware date back to World War I, but the technology necessary to enable a combat aircraft to "see without being seen" would not mature for many decades.

Some of the earliest functional applications of low observables (LO) technology were incorporated into the A-12/SR-71 family of high-altitude reconnaissance jets and the Advanced Manned Strategic Aircraft (AMSA) initiative that ultimately produced the B-1 bomber. But, in both cases Stealth attributes took a back seat to LO's natural enemy, aerodynamic performance. These were not dedicated Stealth platforms.

It wasn't until Lockheed's Advanced Development Projects office — better known as the "Skunk Works" — landed a contract for DARPA's (Defense Advanced Research Projects Agency) XST program (experimental, Stealth, tactical) in 1974 that an aircraft design would feature Stealth as its primary driver. The resulting production bird, the F-117A Stealth fighter, was first delivered to the Air Force in October 1983. Some 50 F-117s have since been consolidated into the 4450th Tactical Air Group operating out of Nellis AFB, Nevada, though uncomfirmed sightings have been reported from England to Japan.

Germination of the Family Tree

The Department of Defense (DoD) release of a heavily re-touched photo of the F-117A brought one of the blackest of the black programs out of the closet. But the public relations-inspired move was something of a false start for Stealthwatchers, as the image did not conform to their expectations, and served to pose more questions than it answered. To make matters worse, DoD was not about to give out any but the sketchiest technical details on the odd looking little fighter.

The most stunning revelation to be divined from the photo concerns the physical nature of the aircraft itself: rather than exhibiting the highly-blended, svelte form favored by imaginative Stealth artists, the F-117 was revealed to be a boxy, deltoid hybrid flying wing with twin "V" tail fins tacked on in such a way that they almost appear to be an afterthought (which — based on the concept of the flying wing design, and reports of the F-117's unstable flight characteristics — they may very well have been). In fact, the fuselage is "blended" with the wing surface only in the most liberal application of the term, as the engine nacelles which straddle it create a non-uniform stepped blending of sorts.

The F-117 may appear homely to the armchair jet-jockey, but the eminently stealthy, single-seat strike fighter is beautiful to the real-life zoomies charged with suppressing hardened enemy C3 bunkers, SAM sites and other high-value targets that lie far beyond the FLOT (Forward Line of Own Troops) in well-defended rear areas.

Nuts and Bolts

As a first-generation dedicated Stealth aircraft, the F-117 isn't quite as "high speed" as the recently revealed Northrop B-2 bomber (second generation) or third generation types like the Advanced Tactical Fighter (ATF) and Advanced Tactical Aircraft (ATA).

For example, the radar absorbent material (RAM) used to sheath the fuselage is of a non-structural variety which takes the form of flat, polygonal applique tiles. Just as a finely-faceted jewel reflects beams of light, the multitudinous angles of these RAM tiles, as well as every other angle incorporated into the F-117 design, are carefully arranged to send unabsorbed radar waves away from their source, regardless of its relative position to the Stealth fighter.

Contrary to previous conjecture, there are virtually no curves on the F-117 — even the fully-faired canopy is flat-surfaced and faceted (as opposed to the one-piece bubble type typically illustrated). However, the incompatibility of most passive RAM natures with transparent applications would render flat canopy panels a veritable beacon to radar. This suggests the incorporation of some active form of RAM — the circuit analog variety, perhaps, which creates a radar-defeating electrically-charged field. This approach "kills two birds with one stone." While it keeps enemy radar from penetrating the cockpit, it also prevents the escape of internal emissions — such as those generated by communications gear, CRTs, or digital flight controls.

The nose section and leading edges of the tail fins and wings (which are planar rather than radically anhedral, as had been supposed) feature a non-reflective, heat-absorbent substance developed by the U.S. Air Force (USAF)

Materials Laboratory at Wright-Patterson AFB, Ohio. The Dow Chemical composite creation, Fibaloy (a proprietary boron fiber/polymer prepreg material), is said to be used extensively in load-bearing components such as spars, ribs and longerons.

Multi-strake, low profile air intakes and serpentine ducting feed the F-117's dual General Electric (GE) F404 turbofan engines. Somewhat modified from their original low-bypass progenitors, these F404s have been refanned to elevate them to a high-bypass status, and afterburners have been eliminated to reduce the ambient thermal signature.

The Stealth fighter's IR (infrared) profile has been further reduced by cooling and baffling the exhaust, which is ultimately diffused into the atmosphere through dorsal louvered nozzles. The tail fins — typically considered to be radar reflectors of the first degree — are constructed primarily of composite materials to minimize telltale radar sidelobes, while their oblique angles further contribute to rendering them nearly invisible to inquisitive electronics.

A sophisticated avionics suite, highlighted by a digital fly-by-wire system, was provided under subcontract by Lear Siegler, while Westinghouse shouldered responsibility for the F-117's power generation/management system. Little technical detail can be verified regarding the highly-classified and all-important ECM package, but suffice it to say that it is far more complex and effective in "spoofing" enemy radar than any other operational system.

Name of the Game

Lockheed's effort to achieve all-aspect stealthiness has not been without purpose, for rather than soaring at Mach 3 within the safe haven of ultra-high altitude flight, or clinging to terrain contours via nap-of-the-earth (NOE) techniques, the F-117 is restricted to whispering along undetected at subsonic speeds in the incredibly vulnerable envelope that lies between.

It is the F-117's benign flight profile — coupled with inherently good aerodynamics (thanks, in part, to an absence of external stores) and multiple fuel cells tucked neatly into every square centimeter of surplus internal space — that yields a combat radius which is indeed commendable for a jet of its size. This extended range is a critical feature for a tactical aircraft with a deep strike/interdiction mission, and it is further enhanced by an air-to-air refueling capability.

As a strike aircraft with a very specific mission and limited ordnance capacity (two internal stations), the F-117 is not armed for dogfighting. If its stealth attributes function as advertised, it won't need to be. Its weapon of choice is the BLU-109/B warhead mated with the Paveway III laser-guided penetration bomb. This is readily deduced by the fact that the BLU-109 is admirably suited to the F-117's mission and, further, the Air Force refuses to indicate what unit or units are receiving this weapon (which narrows the field a bit). The AGM-65D MAVERICK would also prove an effective partner, as would the AGM-88 HARM (High Speed Anti-Radiation Missile). Other weapon systems could be teamed with the F-117A as dictated by the nature of the intended target.

The Stealth fighter's dual mission is clearly defined: the surgical neutralization of hardened and/or high-value targets, or the covert collection of low-altitude photographic intelligence. Its minimal payload is nonetheless sufficient to allow the Stealth fighter to dispatch Soviet SAM sites before they even know what hit them, thereby sanitizing a

corridor for its high-profile, heavily-armed comrades to exploit. Thanks to its imperceptibility, the Stealth fighter can tackle a wide variety of targets — key bridges and rail head, power plants, fuel dumps...the list goes on.

Conceived to augment conventional fighters, the F-117A is unique in that it is a one-man/one-plane/one-mission system. As there aren't many of them, the wing commander must make every bird count. He dares not risk them against any but the most high-value targets, whose hardened nature or formidable defenses preclude the use of any other type of manned offensive weapon system.

Not since World War I has that rare breed of aviator, the Lone Wolf, taken to the skies. But the introduction of the F-117A has changed all that, for rather than being a triumph of technology over humanity, the Stealth fighter embodies a reaffirmation of faith in the white silk scarf flier.

Stealth: The Second Generation

The second black program to be unveiled, Northrop's B-2 Stealth bomber, rolled out of a huge hangar at the contractor's Palmdale plant for a limited public viewing on November 22, 1988.

A lineal descendant of Jack Northrop's functional flying wing of the late 1940s, the B-2 has a massive wingspan of 172 feet. Based on its somewhat bulbous appearance when viewed head-on, coupled with its long-range penetration mission, it may very well sport a maximum takeoff weight of approximately 350,000 pounds!

The vestigial fuselage offers considerable internal volume for fuel, avionics and ordnance, the latter being housed in twin side-by-side Advanced Applications Rotary Launchers of eight weapons each. Despite pundits' insistence that the B-2's mission is strictly one of nuclear first-strike retaliation, the Air Force contends that it has a much broader job description in mind.

Naturally, Soviet mobile ICBM launchers would constitute one primary target, but conventional strikes are also on the agenda. A weapon selection which includes the B83 nuclear gravity bomb and the AGM-129 Advanced Cruise Missile (ACM) would be tailored to a mission picked from the constantly updated National Strategic Target List, a catalog of some 50,000 potential targets.

Originally intended for high-altitude penetration exclusively, a mid-term redesign has rendered the B-2 capable of operating in the low-altitude envelope as well. This dual capability was a late call by the Air Force, deemed necessary by the fact that the B-2 will ultimately assume the duties of the controversial B-1B.

A Growing Family

As odd as it may seem, the still highly-classified F-117A strike fighter represents 15-year-old Stealth technology. Though it was unveiled only two weeks later, the B-2 — the largest aircraft ever constructed primarily of non-metallic materials — is actually much closer to state-of-the-art in the LO arena.

As previously mentioned, yet another generation of stealthy fliers is on the drawing boards. The two projects which fall into the Gen III catagory are the Navy's ATA, slated to replace the A-6 Intruder, and the Air Force ATF, viewed as successor for the vaunted F-15.

Under a 1986 initiative aimed at increasing interservice cooperation, the USAF has agreed to consider the ATA as a potential replacement for its F-111 variable-geometry strike fighter while, for their part, Navy planners have given the nod to the ATF to supplant their own fleet of swing-wing F-14s.

Some defense analysts insist that there is sufficient evidence to suggest that the USAF is also pursuing a black program to develop a follow-on reconnaissance aircraft for the SR-71 Blackbird under the code name "Aurora." Finally, in addition to the systems designed to be flown by human pilots, LO technology has been incorporated into unmanned air vehicles (UAV) as well. Perhaps the best example of this species is the AGM-136 Tacit Rainbow anti-radiation UAV/missile system.

In conclusion, this overview of three, and possibly four, generations of aerial Stealth platforms makes one thing quite clear: as the search for enhanced LO continues at breakneck pace, there will probably never be another military aircraft designed without a great deal of thought being given to its ability to achieve that most highly cherished of all combat assets — surprise. IDA

Northrop B-2 bomber during roll-out ceremonies.

Since the fuel crisis during the early 1970s, and increasingly tight defense budgets, the need to reduce the operating costs of military aircraft has become ever more pressing. Never more so than in the field of pilot training, where a substantial proportion of the huge and growing cost of training fast jet pilots is due to flying time on basic and advanced trainers and on conversion training on front line aircraft. It was against this background that British Aerospace (BAe), then called Hawker Siddeley Aviation, began to explore the possibility of building a trainer to replace the Royal Air Force's (RAF) aging fleet of Gnats and Hunters in the advanced flying and tactical weapons training roles.

The RAF was well aware of the need both to replace these aircraft and to create a systematic approach to pilot training in which the learning curve was kept as steep as the student could bear, and the operating costs of a large and diverse fleet of training aircraft was reduced. Air Staff Requirement 397 sets out the basic requirements for a new advanced flying and weapons trainer. Following a competitive evaluation of several design proposals, in 1971 the RAF selected Hawker Siddeley's P.1182 design. The aircraft was to be called the Hawk TMk1. A contract was awarded by the United Kingdom (UK) Ministry of Defence (MoD) for one pre-production and 175 production aircraft for the Royal Air Force. A conventional design, the Hawk is a tandem-seat transonic advanced flying and weapons trainer powered by a Rolls-Royce Adour Mk151 turbofan engine.

The Hawk was designed with improved reliability and ease of maintenance in mind. With its simple design and inherent strength, the Hawk was able to provide the low operating costs and high utilization that would enable a succession of foreign military customers to update their flight training programs. With many other types of training aircraft, especially older ones, the flight training takes more time. In addition, students face a lengthy and expensive conversion course to front line aircraft on completion of their training. Because it can train pilots in weapons delivery and tactical flying techniques, the Hawk eliminates a great deal of operational conversion flying time. To date 11 air arms on four continents have ordered the Hawk as a trainer and, in some cases, as an operational front line aircraft.

HAWK
MORE THAN A TRAINER

by Terry Treadwell

The first customer to receive the Hawk, in 1976, was No. 4 Flying Training School at RAF Valley in North Wales. From the outset, the Hawk appeared to be virtually ideal from the servicing aspect. Accessibility was the keyword. One man could carry out a turnaround between sorties in less than 10 minutes. An engine change could be achieved in one and three quarter hours, compared to the Hunter and Gnat, which took up to three days. Overall, the Hawk has seen a cut in defect rates of nearly 75 percent, maintenance man hour savings of 50 percent and, through fuel economy alone, a reduction in running costs of nearly 45 percent.

Student pilots who fly the Hawk will have been selected for fast jet training, preparing to fly the Tornado, Jaguar, Harrier, Buccaneer or Phantom operationally, after careful streaming according to their abilities and aptitudes.

The initial pilot training, after which students are divided into multi-engine rotary wing and fast jet streams, involves a 33-week, 76-hour course on the Jet Provost 3A or 5A. Those selected for fast jets do a further 15-week flying training course in which they spend 58 hours on the Jet Provost as an introduction to the Hawk. On completion of this course, they go to RAF Valley for a 22-week advanced flying course on the Hawk in which they fly 75 hours in the aircraft (25 of them solo) and 21 hours in the simulator. The average student usually solos in the Hawk after about 9 hours. It takes an additional 20 hours dual and 11 hours solo flying to convert to type. The rest of the course is made up of instrument flying, night flying, navigation training, low level exercises over extremely difficult terrain and close formation and tactical flying. On successful completion of the Valley course, the pilot is awarded his wings.

In 1977, No 1 Tactical Weapons Unit (TWU) at RAF Brawdy in South Wales accepted delivery of its first Hawk TMk1s, followed by No. 2 TWU at RAF Chivenor in Devon. Unlike the Valley aircraft, which are flown "clean," the TWU Hawks have fuselage and wing pylons to carry a 30mm Aden gun pod on the centerline and a variety of air-to-ground stores, such as rockets and practice bombs, under the wings. During the early 1980s, the RAF ordered British Aerospace to modify the TWU Hawks to carry AIM-9 SIDEWINDER air-to-air missiles for use in the defense of airfields and vital installations during wartime. The modified Hawks, designated TMk1A, are flown by TWU instructors in the Mixed Fighter Force (MFF) role, alongside Phantoms or Tornados to provide extra firepower for Britain's air defenses.

The paint scheme of the TWU Hawks differs from that of the Valley aircraft. The original matt polyurethane green/grey camouflage of the weapon-training aircraft is being replaced with a light air defense grey scheme for the MFF role. The Valley aircraft are painted for high visibility in gloss acrylic signal red, white and pale grey.

The TWU teaches the newly qualified pilots the combat tactics and weapon delivery procedures currently used by the RAF's operational fighters. Visibility from both front and rear seats is excellent, enabling the instructor, in the initial stages, to supervise the student's weapon aiming through a second gunsight fitted in the rear cockpit. Most of the flying, however, is carried out solo, although frequently accompanied by an instructor in another Hawk.

The TWU course lasts a total of 54 flying hours (18 dual, 36 solo) in 64 sorties over 16 weeks. It is only then that the pilot is ready to convert to the aircraft he will fly operationally. The final step to front line flying is a course at the type's Operational Conversion Unit (OCU), which may last up to 75 hours. For example, pilots assigned to a Tornado spend about 40 hours at the Tri-national Tornado Training Establishment (TTTE) at RAF Cotttesmore, Leicestershire, and another 30 hours at the Tornado Weapons

Conversion Unit at RAF Honington.

The highest accolade to be paid to the Hawk TMk1 came in 1979 when the RAF Aerobatic Display Team, the Red Arrows, chose the aircraft to replace their aging Gnats. These Hawks, too, were upgraded to TMk1A standard. The only difference between them and standard TWU aircraft is the more powerful Adour Mk861-2 engine with an accelerator switch modification, a fuel-cooled oil cooler and a Magnavox ARC-164 UHF radio.

One other school is equipped with three Hawk TMk1s: the Empire Test Pilot's School (ETPS) at RAF Boscomb Down, where some of the finest test pilots in the world are trained. The Hawks will eventually replace the two-seat Hunter TMk7s which, among other things, are used to teach students recovery techniques from inverted spins. Additional instrumentation is fitted to these Hawks, mainly for downlinking flight test information to a ground pilot for later use in analysis and presentation exercises. The only noticeable external distinction is the fitment of Alpha and Beta vanes on the nose pitot tube. One of the Hawks, however, has been fitted with a variable

stability system developed by the Cranfield Institute of Technology for ETPS to replace the aging Beagle Bassett now being used.

The main features of the variable stability Hawk are a digital computer, a system controller, a flight safety monitor and primary flight control actuators. The instructor sits in the rear cockpit where his controls are physically connected to the aircraft's primary control surfaces, as in the standard aircraft. The student's controls, however, are connected through the computer, thus enabling the instructor to program the Hawk's flight envelope to represent the handling characteristics of other aircraft, for example, the varying wing sweep angles of the Tornado or the stall characteristics of an RAF Tristar tanker. This, of course, is an oversimplification of a very complex computer system, but it allows an insight into the world of test pilot training and the need for trustworthy aircraft with honest, safe and predictable handling characteristics.

We saw the first export order for the Hawk in 1977, when the Finnish Air Force signed a contract for 50 Hawk Mk51s to replace its aging Fouga Magisters. The first four

aircraft were built in Kingston, and the remainder were assembled by Valmet in Finland. Powered by the Adour Mk851 engine, this variant had a 70 percent greater payload, 30 percent greater range and a 30 percent greater takeoff weight than the TMk1. Other minor variations include the fitting of the SAAB RGS-2 gunsight and a 12.7mm VKT-42 gun in place of the 30mm Aden.

The Hawk Mk52 was selected by the Kenyan Air Force in 1978. It was the first to be equipped with a brake parachute and the two extra weapon pylons under the wings that all subsequent export Hawks carry. Later that year, the Indonesian Air Force ordered the first of 20 Hawk Mk53s eventually delivered for advanced flying and weapons training. The first flight of the Indonesian Air Force Hawk Mk53 was on June 6, 1980, with the first delivery to Jogjakarta Air Force base in September of that year. The Zimbabwe Air Force ordered eight Hawk Mk60s in January 1981 for both training and combat duties. The Mk61 was ordered by the Dubai Air Wing of the United Arab Emirates Air Force later that same year.

The first of a new series of Hawks, the 100 series, made its maiden flight on October 21, 1987. Similar in many respects to the 60-series aircraft, the Hawk 100 has an extended nose to carry advanced navigation and attack avionics, including a Forward Looking Infra Red (FLIR) and laser rangefinder. The aircraft will be fitted with advanced, digital instrumentation and a head-up display (HUD), radar warning receiver, HOTAS (hands on throttle and stick) controls and an inertial navigation system (INS). Used as a systems management trainer, the Hawk 100 will prepare pilots for the highly advanced supersonic aircraft fitted with state-of-the-art avionics which they will fly in operational squadrons, thus reducing as far as possible the increasing cost of conversion flying on sophisticated front line aircraft. Fitted with the same more powerful Adour Mk871 engine and advanced combat wing as the single-seat Hawk 200 fighter, the Hawk 100 will have all the "feel" of a front line jet with the running costs of a trainer. On top of all that, it is a very capable fighter and ground attack aircraft in its own right!

HAWK 100 SERIES

The real export breakthrough came when BAe, partnered with McDonnell Douglas, beat off seven other competitors to win a contract to supply the U.S. Navy with 300 aircraft as part of a complete training package for fast jet pilots known as the T45 Training System (T45TS). McDonnell Douglas is the prime contractor, with Honeywell providing simulators and British Aerospace serving as a partner and prime subcontractor for the T-45A Goshawk (U.S. Navy version). The Goshawk is basically a Hawk 60-series which has been fitted with an arrestor hook and a strengthened airframe and undercarriage to withstand the shock of arrested landings on aircraft carriers and catapult launches.

Although this was a major contract, BAe still had other commitments to meet. In 1982 the first deliveries were made to Zimbabwe and Dubai while, in 1983, the Abu Dhabi Air Force ordered 16 Hawk Mk63s to join Dubai's aircraft in the inventory of the United Arab Emirates Air Force. Later that year, Kuwait ordered 12 Hawk Mk64s, making the Arab world the biggest Hawk purchaser outside the United States.

PILATUS PC-9

In 1986, the Kingdom of Saudi Arabia signed a Memorandum of Understanding (MoU) with the United Kingdom Government covering the purchase of 132 aircraft. This included 70 Tornados, 30 Hawk Mk65s and 30 Pilatus PC-9 trainers. The Pilatus connection arose from the earlier RAF competition for a turboprop trainer to replace the elderly Jet Provosts.

BAe had teamed up with Pilatus for this competition to offer the PC-9, and although the RAF contract was awarded to Shorts of Belfast, builder of the Embraer Tucano under license, the PC-9 was highly impressive. Both BAe and the Royal Saudi Air Force viewed it as an ideal stepping stone to the Hawk during flying training.

In October 1987, the Swiss Air Force ordered 20 Hawk Mk66 trainers to replace its 40-year-old BAe (de Havilland) Vampires. This contract included a Rediffusion Hawk flight simulator together with a logistic and training package and a license agreement whereby the first aircraft would be delivered by BAe at the end of 1989; the remainder would be built jointly by BAe and Swiss industry with final assembly in Switzerland.

The latest chapter in the Hawk story unfolded in July 1988 when Saudi Arabia signed another MoU with Britain for more aircraft. Press reports suggest that the Royal Saudi Air Force may buy up to 60 extra Hawks, some of which will be single-seat Hawk 200s. Neither BAe nor the UK Ministry of Defence have confirmed any of this speculation, but it would seem that orders and requirements for the Hawk in all its forms have climbed over the 700 mark — an impressive figure for an aircraft which has only been in service for 13 years! IDA

The Hawk TMk1 in various configurations: (top to bottom) Red Arrows Demonstration Team, New Camouflage, Old Camouflage, RAF Valley Trainer. (Below) T45A Goshawk.

PAMPA
IA63

by Terry Treadwell

It was like a meeting of David and Goliath when the Argentina company FMA (Fabrica de Materiales Aeroespaciales) was invited by the United States, to demonstrate its new jet trainer, the IA63 Pampa, to the U.S. Air Force (USAF). The Goliaths were the BAe Hawk, German Alpha Jet, McDonnell Douglas/BAe Goshawk, MB 339, S-211, CASA 101, Pilatus PC-9 and PC-7, Tucano and Squalus. All of these aircraft had proven track records and most were already in service with their respective countries. The question was: what made the Pampa different from all the others? According to General Ruben Corradetti, President of FMA, "The

IA63 features designs and performance characteristics not yet achieved by most other types of aircraft in this category. This is a low-cost, high performance jet trainer with the highest level of reliability and maintainability, and we believe that this is a strong competitor for the replacement of the USAF's T-37."

The IA63 Pampa is a joint venture between FMA of Argentina and Dornier of West Germany. Both companies have a history of producing good aircraft, but this partnership will be a test for the skills of both companies in the competition. The first Latin-American jet was created by FMA in 1947. It was the single-seat fighter, the IA27 Pulqui

I. This was followed in 1950 by the IA33 Pulqui II and, more recently, the IA58 Pucara which saw action in the Falkland Islands campaign in 1982.

Although built in Cordoba in the Argentinian Republic, 71 percent of the aircraft's components are produced in the United States, encompassing more than 30 states. This includes the Garrett TFE 731 turbofan engine which is manufactured in Phoenix, Arizona.

The Pampa is a single-engine, high-wing monoplane, with a tandem two-seat cockpit and a retractable tricycle undercarriage. Its primary function is that of a high performance military jet trainer, to be used for basic pilot training and

IA63 FMA Pampa Specifications:

Wing Span	31 ft. 9 in.	Max Cruise	464 mph/sea level.
Wing Area	168 sq. ft.	Climb Rate	5,315 ft. /minute
L.O.A.	35 ft. 9 in.	Service Ceiling	42,325 ft.
H.O.A.	14 ft. 1 in.	Range	930 miles/345 mph
Engine	Garrett Turbofan	Fuel Capacity	2,560 lbs.
	TFE 731- 2/1X	Weight, Maximum	8,377 lbs.
Max Speed	509 mph	Weight, empty	5,791 lbs.

for advanced flight training. The Pampa program started in 1979, but it was four years before the first prototype took off. The second flew on August 7, 1985, and the third on March 25, 1986. The third prototype differed from the others, having Stencel ejection seats fitted in preference to the Martin-Baker seats. It also had provision to carry armament. The armament consisted of a 30mm centerline pod cannon and four under-wing pylons capable of carrying 640 pounds of ordnance on each.

The aircraft has been cleared for aerobatics and spinning exercises, including the inverted spin. It is said the recovery is made by adopting the "hands-off" procedure.

The IA63 jet trainer has STOL (Short Take Off Landing) capabilities from airstrips that range from a semi-prepared airstrip in a war zone, to a highway or auto route. The avionics consist of a redundant VHF system for radio communications and intercom system. A navigation system consists of one VOR/ILS with MARKER, one DME and one ADF radio compass which allows for complete navigation and landing training under IFR conditions. A three-gyro platform provides the altitude and heading information, while additional heading reference is provided by a magnetic flux valve compass.

The one-piece canopy gives both pilots excellent visibility, and the

stepping arrangement of the tandem seating gives the pilot in the rear seat the impression of being in a single-seat fighter.

As with all cost effective programs, maintenance manhours are of paramount importance. With this in mind, the IA63 Pampa was developed to minimize maintenance manhours per flight hours. This was achieved by making all service and maintenance operations from ground level without the use of ladders or steps. The engine can be changed in less than one hour and the aircraft has a turn around time of 10 minutes. Taken together, the ease of servicing and maintenance means maximum operational availability. IDA

MiG-29

FULCRUM

How Good Is It?

by William Sweetman

Four years ago, even two, nobody would have believed it: a gaggle of four fighters, two Royal Air Force (RAF) Tornado F.3 interceptors flanking a pair of rakish, red-starred Mikoyan-Gurevich MiG-29s. The Tornados broke away as the MiG-29s touched down in formation on Farnborough airfield.

Throughout the first week of the 1988 Farnborough air show, the MiG-29s — one single-seater and a MiG-29UB trainer — drew record crowds to witness a display routine that smacked not only of "glasnost" but also of showmanship. The Soviet party trick — the tailslide — distinguished their demonstrations in the same way as the Harrier's curtsy or the F-16's spiral vertical climb.

That the MiG-29 can fly a good display, there is no doubt. But how good is it as a fighter? How does it compare with the best of the West? Faster? More agile? Better armed?

First, the basics. The MiG-29 is no lightweight. Slightly larger and about 15 percent more powerful than the F/A-18 Hornet, it is substantially bigger than the F-16 or the Mirage 2000. Its basic shape is quite different from any Western fighter, but is not at all unlike that of the contemporary, but much larger, Sukhoi Su-27.

The MiG-29 is almost a "twin-boom" design, like the P-38 Lightning of World War II. The engines and tail assemblies are carried by booms attached to the wing; the aft "fuselage" between them is little more than a web. The fuselage proper is almost a nacelle, projecting forwards and upwards

from the wing. Broad leading edge root extensions (LERXes) extend from a point just behind the radome to the leading edges of the main wing, well aft of the intake lips.

The swept, medium-aspect-ratio wing is thicker than the wings of the F-16 and F-18, making it slightly heavier but improving its ability to carry heavy or awkwardly shaped loads. It is fitted with conventional ailerons and full-span leading edge slats, which form an aerodynamic slot as they open. This helps to stabilize the aircraft at high angles of attack, but slats cause more drag at high speeds than the plain maneuvering flaps fitted to the F-16 and F-18. The broad LERXes and long-span wing promise good maneuverability and turning performance.

With the widest part of the forebody located well ahead of the wing, the configuration achieves one of its main goals: it accommodates the largest radar of any fighter of its size. The antenna of the SO-90 measures some 36 inches in diameter, larger than that of the F/A-18 or Mirage 2000 and greater even than the F-16 dish. A larger antenna translates directly into longer range and better resolution, other things being equal. The radar is backed up by an infrared search and track (IRST) system, which can detect the hot exhaust plumes of military aircraft well beyond visual range; its optical head, projecting from the fuselage ahead of the windshield, is shared by a laser rangefinder for gunnery use.

The MiG-29 is designed in careful accordance with the Area Rule, the aerodynamic principle which guides designers in the reduction of drag at supersonic speeds. According to the Area Rule, the cross-sectional area of the design should vary gradually from nose to tail. The various components of the MiG-29 — forward fuselage, LERXes, engine nacelles and wings — add up to an excellent area profile. Even the

landing gear is affected; rather than thickening the nacelles to accommodate it, the designers gave the MiG-29 a long landing gear which nestles above the inlet ducts inside the wing.

High-speed performance goals are also evident in the sharp-lipped, steeply raked engine inlets with variable internal ramps. Because Vietnam experience appeared to show that high-altitude, high-Mach flight was less important than maneuverability, the designers of the F-16 and F-18 eliminated variable inlets from their designs in favor of lighter fixed, rounded intakes. In the process, however, they accepted a top speed limit between Mach 1.6 and Mach 2.

One reason for accepting fixed air inlets on a fighter is that it is difficult to approach Mach 2 unless the fighter has no weapons on board, in which case the exercise is pointless. However, this question has been addressed in the design of the MiG-29. Its Tumansky R-33D engines are low-bypass turbofans (like the F-18's F404, or the M53 in the Mirage 2000) which maintain thrust well at high speeds. It also has a very high ratio of thrust-to-weight, to overcome the drag of external missiles.

It needs such power, because its armament includes some of the largest air-to-air missiles ever seen. The normal load includes two AA-10 ALAMO semi-active AAMs (air-to-air missile) on the inboard wing pylons. These huge weapons are well over twice as heavy as most Western AAMs; it is hard to say exactly why. A bigger AAM can have a longer-burning motor, improving its terminal maneuverability. Due to its larger diameter, its seeker head can be bigger and more sensitive at a given technology level and it can have a greater warhead, which at a given miss distance might destroy its target rather than merely knocking it out of the fight. A certain conservatism in the design of radar-guided AAMs might not be bad; few of them have ever proved decisive in combat or performed precisely as expected. On the MiG-29, the AA-10 is backed up by up to four short-range AA-8 APEX missiles and a 30mm gun.

The F-16 and F-18 normally carry no more than four missiles. On the F-18, two of these can be radar-guided AIM-7s, but most F-16s are equipped only with the infrared homing AIM-9 SIDEWINDER. Capable though it is, the AIM-9 is limited in range by the atmosphere's absorption of IR energy. Even the AIM-7, in theory, has less range than the massive AA-10. With a bigger radar and longer-ranging missiles, the MiG-29 should have a "first look, first shot" advantage over the F-16 and F-18, at present.

Some features and capabilities of the MiG-29 are simply absent from Western fighters. The biggest surprise for Western observers, when the aircraft made its public debut in Finland in July 1986, was the fact that the aircraft has two air intake systems. When the aircraft lands, a pressure switch on the nosewheel activates a massive pair of doors which seal off the main air intakes, while two sets of large louvre doors open in the upper surface of the LERXes.

This system is a drastic solution to the foreign-object damage (FOD) problem. It is also an expensive

A close look at the MiG-29's twin air intakes and landing gear.

Special air inlets and low pressure tires allow operation from gravel strips or crude runways.

remedy in complexity, weight and internal volume, adding several hundred pounds in dead weight and displacing the equivalent of 1,000 pounds of internal fuel. But, in combination with the fat, low-pressure tires — the main-wheels are vast compared with those of the bigger F-15 — the special inlets allow the MiG-29 to operate from gravel strips or roughly repaired runways, unlike any Western fighter except the AV-8B Harrier.

The MiG-29, therefore, is fast, maneuverable, well equipped and heavily armed. In many basic statistics, it appears superior to all except the top-of-the-line Western fighters such as the F-15C/D. However, there are other important points to be taken into account.

The MiG-29 is a later design than any current Western fighter. The first prototypes were seen in 1978, so the design dates from the mid-1970s, after the main features of all the West's current fighters had been published and discussed. High-rate production started in 1985. By that time, the Western fighters against which the MiG-29 is often assessed were in service in thousands. New fighters such as EFA and Rafale will be equally well armed and more agile, while the USAF's Advanced Tactical

Fighter will also be much faster and — above all — so Stealthy as to be virtually invisible to the MiG's radar. The new AIM-120A AMRAAM missile, emerging from a thicket of technical problems, promises to give both current and future NATO fighters the ability to carry multiple long-range AAMs.

Another vital point about the MiG-29 is that it is part of a mixed force. The Soviet air forces have three modern tactical aircraft to cover missions which some Western forces perform with a single type. Long-range missions such as escorting interdiction/strike aircraft, or breaking up enemy formations over their own territory, can be assigned to the big and expensive Sukhoi Su-27; "mud-mover." Strikes are carried out by the subsonic Su-25.

This leaves the MiG-29 with the classic short-to-medium-range fighter mission: flying top cover for Su-25s, waiting to pounce on any aircraft which may challenge the attackers, theater air defense, or attacking hostile strike aircraft and their escorts.

The MiG-29 is the latest in a long line of MiG fighters to assume this role. The first was the MiG-21, conceived as the minimum fighter which could attain Mach 2 and carry a pair of IR-homing AAMs. It was

followed by the swing-wing MiG-23, which took the MiG-21's positive attributes — its speed and basic simplicity — but was much bigger, so that it could carry a long-range radar/missile suite and still offer a dramatic increase in range.

In the same way, Soviet planners started with the best characteristics of the MiG-23 when they drew up the requirement for its successor. The MiG-29 carries a similarly sized radar and carries a similar mix of weapons, and has equal or better speed and acceleration.

The MiG-29 represents a quantum advance over the MiG-23 is in areas where the NATO air forces have changed since the MiG-23 was designed. In the air- to-air regime, combat experience had shown that long-range missile attacks alone were usually indecisive against fighters, and that the combat usually evolved into a subsonic dogfight. The West's answer, manifested in the design of the F-16 and F-18, was to downplay the importance of long-range missiles in favor of the more reliable IR weapons, in a smaller, cheaper fighter.

But, at the same time, NATO introduced a number of strike aircraft which could find and hit targets from very low altitudes, either in clear weather (Jaguar and

Harrier) or in any conditions (F-111 and Tornado). The Soviets' dilemma was that an F-16-type fighter could not perform their air-defense mission against the emerging low-level threat. At low level, the fighter cannot use its supersonic speed or agility. The answer was to equip all fighters with a pulse-Doppler "look-down, shoot-down" (LDSD) radar which can break targets out of the ground clutter, and a new semi-active homing missile.

Radar, in particular, is a tremendous influence on airplane size as its diameter dictates the size of the forward fuselage, which strongly influences drag. The laws of aerodynamics and the principles of aircraft design are the same at Ramenskoye as they are at Edwards AFB, California. If you want to combine a MiG-23's range and

high top speed with an LDSD radar/missile combination and sustained 9 G capability, the result is a fighter at least as big as an F-15, and comparably costly by any criteria; certainly not something which could be produced on anything along the scale as the MiG-23.

The Soviet solution was a mixed force; less than half its total numbers would be accounted for by superior, long-range fighters for strike escort and offensive counter-air missions — Su-27s. The balance would be a less expensive aircraft tailored to the needs of the frontal air battle, the MiG-29.

This is the key to the puzzling contradictions in the MiG-29's design. It is designed to meet the most critical requirements — speed, acceleration, agility, LDSD armament and front line operability — as

cheaply as possible. To this end, qualities of secondary importance have been virtually ignored.

Range is one of those less important qualities. More powerful than the F-18, the MiG-29 has significantly less room for internal fuel, with its slender mid-section. The auxiliary inlet system occupies a significant amount of external space. As a result, the MiG-29 cannot fly as far as the Western fighters. This is not to condemn the design, but to note that long range was not part of the requirement.

Electronically signaled flight controls (fly-by-wire) have been adopted for Western fighters because they save weight and make the aircraft less difficult to fly in combat; the pilot has less need to keep his eye on the alpha (angle of attack) gauge. The MiG-29 gets by

The MiG-29 Fulcrum (above) is a formidable adversary for current Western fighters, including (clockwise at left) the F/A-18, F-15E, F-3 Tornado, Mirage 2000, F-14A and F-16C.

with conventional mechanically signaled controls and a stability-augmentation system (which limits the aircraft's responsiveness towards the corners of the envelope). The result is some loss of high-end agility and an absence of the "carefree" handling that distinguishes such Western fighters as the F-16, Mirage 2000 and F-18. The MiG-29 pilot will have to fight with one eye on his alpha gauge, redlined at 25 degrees. The famous tailslide indicates confidence in the engines' stall resistance. While it may be one way of breaking a Doppler track, it would certainly be an incredibly stupid tactic anywhere near a hostile fighter, leaving the MiG-29 hanging in the sky, out of airspeed and control authority.

Fighter pilots and former fighter pilots play an important role in the definition of Western fighters. In the late 1960s, the pilot community demanded, and won, a return to the cockpit visibility they had enjoyed in the days of the P-51 Mustang and F-86 Sabre. Both fighters have immense canopies, with sills below shoulder level. Not so in the Soviet Union. Fighter tactics stress the offensive. The MiG-29 is faster than its likely opponents, and cockpit visibility requirements are thus stringent only in the forward hemisphere. To reduce drag, the MiG-29 has been fitted with a narrow, high-silled canopy which gives the

pilot no room to turn his head. Mirrors provide rear vision.

Likewise, the improvements which have been made inside Western fighter cockpits are not reflected in the MiG-29, which has a low-technology, easily maintained arrangement of conventional dial and tape instruments and warning lights. The panel is cluttered, and the old type instruments relegate vital information such as the radar-warning receiver (RWR) display to the lower corners of the panel. The head-up display (HUD) is similar to 1960s Western designs, and lacks the up-front control (UFC) panel which allows Western pilots to reprogram their displays and enter system commands without taking their eyes off the outside world.

The most advanced feature of the cockpit, apparently, is the helmet-mounted display (HMD). This has not been shown in the West. We do not know, for instance, how the pilot's head movements are tracked or how much information is displayed on the helmet. Even simple HMDs have been shown to be useful in "cueing" the pilot to a target detected by radar or an IRST, or in indicating to the pilot whether a target is within missile range.

It can be argued that what is missing from the MiG-29 is the gold plate; pilot amenities such as all-round visibility, gimmicky displays, or extra range, which will be

needed on only a few missions best handled by a smaller force of long-range fighters.

If you look at the design in the context of Soviet tactics, this is probably correct. Even in the early 1970s, Soviet fighter doctrine was the antithesis of Manfred von Richthofen's famous words: "The fighter pilots would have an allotted area to cruise around in as it suits them, but when they have an opponent they must attack and shoot him down. Anything else is absurd." Any Soviet pilot who "cruised around as it suited him" would have been in deep trouble. Fighters were vectored on to specific targets by ground control, attacked in a single pass and escaped to land, refuel and re-arm.

Modern Soviet tactics permit the pilot more autonomy, but there is still a gap between Soviet and Western doctrine and training. The MiG-29 is designed for ground-vectored intercepts; the targets will have been detected and identified on the ground or by airborne control aircraft. The purpose of the radar and IRST is to help the pilot carry out the attack, not to search out and select targets. Because the pilot is in constant touch with ground control, his navigation and mission-management tasks are less complicated (he does not have to enter new waypoints in flight, for example) so the absence of multipurpose instruments is less important.

The tailslide maneuver reflects confidence in the MiG-29's ability to resist engine stalls.

The combat itself starts with a maximum-range missile attack, which destroys several of the enemy aircraft and disrupts their formation, followed by a short, high-energy, close-range missile and gun attack to claim additional victims. Before the hostiles can regroup and reclaim the initiative, the MiG-29 pilot uses his high acceleration to "get out of Dodge." Throughout, the emphasis is on high speed and acceleration to maintain the initiative, avoid defensive fights and to disengage at will.

Much of the difference between the MiG-29 and Western fighters can be summed up in one word: flexibility. In a fast, slash-and-turn attack against identified, designated targets, the MiG-29 is a formidable opponent. But as you move away from that "design point," there are features of the MiG-29 that could prove less desirable. If the nature of the combat changes rapidly in flight, the MiG-29 pilot is going to be head-down and scribbling on his kneepad while his Western adversary punches a rapid sequence on his MFDs and up-front control. If the controllers have erred badly or been spoofed, he may be low on fuel before he can divert to another part of the battle zone.

If beyond-visual-range (BVR) target identification is not fully reliable, the BVR missiles become much less useful. And if the BVR attack is indecisive, or blunted by jamming, the MiG-29 pilot is at an increasing disadvantage as the combat breaks up into a Mach 0.9 furball and his rear sectors fill with hostiles. At that point, all-round visibility is no longer a luxury. More than half the surviving victims of fighter-versus-fighter attacks report that they never saw their attacker.

The history of air combat tells us that such "ifs" are not only possible, but virtual certainties. Many people have tried to answer the question, "How good is the MiG-29" in terms of its speed, its armament, or even the way it is built. As we have seen, the real issues are more complex. Classic fighters are more than collections of statistics or a sum of their parts. IDA

TAC
The Fighter Team
by Joe Poyer

Fly, Fight, Win — three words that summarize the mission of the Tactical Air Command (TAC). As with all combat elements, it is the team approach that makes TAC work.

It may seem strange to talk about a "team" when dealing with a branch of the Air Force whose primary task is one-on-one aerial combat. A popular perception of the fighter pilot has emerged from Hollywood movies, dramatizing "lone eagles" who roar off into the dawn to do battle in their sleek jets. While some may be steely-eyed warriors, they do not fly alone. The fighter pilot is only one member of the team.

"TAC trains their pilots to go anywhere, anytime, take on and beat any adversary," said Major Ian Milne, Assistant Operations Officer for the 63rd Tactical Training Squadron (TTS), MacDill Air Force Base (AFB), Florida. But, Maj. Milne also pointed out that, "the pilot depends on the support of many other Air Force personnel."

Without the Aircraft Maintenance Unit (AMU), the aircraft won't fly; without Flight Operations, the aircraft won't be available; and without the Security team's watchfulness, the enemy could destroy the aircraft before the pilot reaches the cockpit.

THE PILOT

It has been said that good pilots are born, not made. Nevertheless, all pilots need training. A TAC pilot follows an intricate and lengthy path to reach the cockpit of an operational fighter squadron. Following completion of Officer Candidate School (OCS), the Reserve Officer's Training Corps (ROTC) program or gradu-ation from the U.S. Air Force Academy, the new pilot passes through a minimum of 18 months of intensive flight training and academic work. Student pilots are not strangers to book work; all are college graduates.

In training, student pilots spend hours in simulators, flight trainers and bent over desks studying well into the early morning hours as they struggle through what seems an impossible work load.

They become fighter pilots for many reasons, but most are motivated by one in particular; they enjoy the heady sense of independence and power that comes from controlling a Mach 2 aircraft carrying more firepower than an entire World War II fighter squadron.

Specially trained Security Police are responsible for air base ground defense and for flight line security. No one without the proper authorization comes onto the flight line. Air Force security personnel specializing in air base ground defense are highly trained, combat-ready troops.

TAC FLIGHT PROFILE

A TAC fighter mission can be divided into four broad phases: mission planning briefing, preflight, flight and debriefing. Whether the mission is training or operational, all flights include all four phases, and each of the elements in the fighter squadron is intimately involved.

Preflight — The AMU works through the night to ready the aircraft for the next day's work, planned as much as a month before. As one shift goes off, another comes on duty. The departing production supervisor briefs the incoming one on the number of aircraft that are flightworthy. They discuss in detail unresolved problems.

"Each fighter aircraft has assigned to it a specific crew chief who is responsible for that aircraft's airworthiness," according to Staff Sergeant John Swann, a crew chief in the 61st AMU. He noted that "Form 781 has the maintenance history of the aircraft, and is their 'bible'. It is the crew chief's responsibility to see that the aircraft is flightworthy and that all reported problems have been resolved — right down to refueling and a clean canopy."

Only when the crew chief is satisfied will the aircraft be reported to the AMU's expediter as "crew ready." The expediter, in turn, reports to the duty production supervisor, who notifies Flight Operations. The aircraft is then moved to the parking ramp.

Briefing — The student pilots and their instructors, or operational pilots, scheduled for missions arrive two hours prior to flight time to begin their Preflight Mission Briefing. By this time, Operations has established the number of flightworthy aircraft. The Air Force strictly enforces a 12-hour work day on flight crews to ensure that they receive sufficient rest.

Training mission briefings are generally longer than operational mission preflight briefings. The student is concerned not only with the day's lesson, but must master related material called out in the course syllabus as well.

If, for instance, the TAC student pilot will be practicing BFM10s, the head-to-head pass which is a basic fighter maneuver, the instructor will spend a great deal of time going over the fundamentals and fine points of the lesson. They discuss how to maneuver into shooting position, what rates of speed to use, right and left turns, how to set the switches for radar lock-on, and weapons selection.

Instructors usually arrive ahead of their students. Beyond training responsibilities, the instructor has other duties assigned. According to Instructor Pilot Captain Marshall Formby, "he may have been assigned as a scheduler, a weapons specialist, safety officer or to any of the dozens of tasks that must be performed to keep the squadron operational. And he has to maintain his own proficiency as well."

Preflight Checkout — When the mission planning is over, the pilot draws his flight suit and helmet and proceeds to the flight line. He is met by the crew chief of the aircraft to which he has been assigned about 45 minutes before flight time. The crew chief accompanies the pilot during the "walk-around" inspec-

tion of the aircraft, and briefs the pilot on any problems specific to this particular aircraft. He then assists the pilot into the cockpit.

Thirty minutes before takeoff, the engines are started and all other equipment powered up. If anything fails to work properly, the pilot reports the situation to the crew chief who is connected to the aircraft by headphones. The crew chief checks the problem. If it is not something that can be resolved easily, the crew chief reports it to the expediter, who relays the information to Operations. A specialist is then dispatched immediately to the flight line. His objective is to fix the problem with the engines still running and the pilot in place. Most problems are repaired in 10 minutes or less. If the problem is severe enough to warrant grounding the aircraft, the production supervisor assigns a spare aircraft and the flight supervisor authorizes the change. The pilot moves to the new aircraft and begins the Preflight checkout from the top.

Standing down an aircraft like the highly automated F-16 Fighting Falcon is becoming a rare occurrence. TAC operational wings recently are averaging a 94 percent mission capable rate.

The crew chief monitors the parts of the aircraft the pilot cannot see from the cockpit, making sure all control surfaces respond and removes all safety pins. If a problem does occur with the engine, the crew chief plugs in a hand-held "data transfer unit" that interrogates the onboard engine monitoring system. The unit can often pinpoint the problem and suggest a solution. If not, the onboard data can be run on a more powerful main frame computer to provide a detailed analysis. After the final brake check, the crew chief pulls the chocks and salutes the pilot.

Flight — To fly, fight and win, the TAC pilot practices endlessly, whether a student, a transitioning pilot, or an operational member of a squadron. While the Navy has its Fighter Weapons School at Miramar Naval Air Station, California, the Air Force has a similar program, the Fighter Weapons School (FWS) at Nellis AFB, Nevada. Pilots are selected from TAC squadrons to attend the FWS for their ability to fly and to communicate to others what they have learned. When pilots complete the FWS and return to their squadrons, they become the designated weapons specialists and are expected to teach their squadron mates the tactics and techniques they have learned.

A modern fighter like the F-16 is an extremely complex aircraft. In many ways, however, because of automation, there is less for the pilot to monitor and control than in earlier aircraft. This allows the pilot to concentrate more closely on using the aircraft as a weapons platform. The pilot fights the aircraft in a "heads up" situation, keeping other aircraft under visual observation at all times. Essential control information such as speed, course, altitude, weapons status, and radar is displayed within his line of sight. Aircraft controls are clustered on the control stick.

Weapons, avionics and computer controls are grouped on a keyed console which the pilot "plays", like a musician. In fact, this unit is often referred to as a piccolo, and pilots must practice the "switches" as diligently as a musician on an instrument.

Most TAC sorties involve at least two aircraft and last between 60 and 90 minutes. In a training flight, a third aircraft may also participate, usually in the aggressor role.

After the aircraft is down and while taxiing to the parking ramp, the pilot radios a preliminary report to the AMU concerning any problems that occurred during the flight. The AMU dis-patches the proper specialists, who talk with the pilot to begin resolving the problem even before he parks the aircraft.

Usually the first person the pilot speaks to, face-to-face, is the aircraft's crew chief who waits with the ladder to help him unstrap and climb out. Invariably, the crew chief's first question is, "How is our aircraft?" - meaning, did you break anything?

Debriefing — Once out of the aircraft, the pilot begins the lengthy debriefing process. First stop is the AMU, where he, the crew chief and the necessary specialists discuss in detail the aircraft's performance and any problems encountered. The AMU's objective is to refuel and rearm the aircraft, effecting any necessary repairs to have it flightworthy as quickly as possible for the next mission. The pilot's first hand account makes it easier to pinpoint problems.

The debriefing continues at squadron operations where the pilot makes detailed written and verbal reports on every aspect of the mission. If it was a training mission, the instructor assesses the student's performance from engine start to shutdown, pointing out mistakes or better ways to accomplish a maneuver. The 56th TTW's F-16s are equipped with video cameras that record exactly what the pilot sees in and through the cockpit. "They offer the greatest help," Lieutenant Larry Miller said of the TV cameras. Miller is undergoing transition training to F-16s. "The pressures on a student pilot are tremendous," he added. "The TV cameras make it very easy to go over the mission in detail, until you understand every mistake you made. Even days later, replaying the tape brings the mission back into sharp focus."

When the debriefing ends, the mission ends. Pilots go on to perform other assigned operational duties and students still face several hours of academic work and even longer hours of homework. But, sooner or later, every pilot will visit the gymnasium to work out. Weightlifting and exercising helps the pilot unwind, and increases his high gravity tolerance.

One of the Wing's most important functions is long range planning as it pertains to scheduling aircraft, personnel and missions. An extremely complicated process at the mercy of high tech equipment, human factors and weather, overall planning is accomplished 30 days in advance.

TAC Headquarters at Langley AFB, Virginia mandates the utilization rate of its aircraft which, in turn, drives the schedule. Every effort is made to keep aircraft in regular service; highly complex electronic and mechanical systems tend to degrade if left unused. Currently, all TAC aircraft must be flown at least once every 21 days.

The local Operations staff establishes the aircraft usage rate 30 days in advance, then "contracts" with maintenance and other functions for their services. This ensures that manpower, equipment and spares will be available when and where needed. If a long range deployment is on the calendar, the AMU is alerted to be ready to accompany their aircraft wherever it goes, with the equipment and spares necessary. The same holds true for Security's ARTs.

TAC is charged with organizing, training, equipping and maintaining a combat-ready force to defend the Continental United States, and to deploy anywhere to meet and defeat any aerial threat.

TAC's three Air Forces are the First, headquartered at Langley AFB, Virginia; the Ninth at Shaw AFB, South Carolina; and the Twelfth at Bergstrom AFB, Texas.

Additional major units are the Tactical Air Warfare Center, Eglin AFB, Florida; the Tactical Fighter Weapons Center, Nellis AFB, Nevada; and the 28th Air Division, Tinker AFB, Oklahoma.

From the Aircraft Maintenance Unit to Flight Operations to Security to the pilot, TAC air operations have been, and will always remain, team operations in which one element is as important as another. It is the team approach that makes the TAC mission of "Fly, Fight, Win" a reality. IDA

European Fighter Competition

by Malcom Lowe

Developing a new fighter aircraft is a difficult, often very lengthy and extremely costly process. Design concepts for a new generation of fighters are already on the drawing boards, with new aircraft set to enter service during the next decade. In Western Europe, the quest for a new fighter has seen the appearance of two principal but very distinct projects. They reflect two particular approaches to the challenge of fighter aircraft design and production.

One of these two major European fighter programs is the European Fighter Aircraft (EFA). This program illustrates the increasing trend in the West, and particularly within Western Europe, towards development of a new combat aircraft as a multinational, fully collaborative project which includes a number of otherwise independent manufacturers. The companies involved in the EFA program are British Aerospace (Great Britain), MBB teamed with Dornier (West Germany), CASA (Spain), and Aeritalia (Italy).

In June 1986, the Munich-based company Eurofighter GmbH was formed as the focus of the EFA project. Shortly afterwards, Eurojet Turbo GmbH was formed to coordinate the design and manufacture of a new advanced turbofan engine to power the EFA — the Eurojet EJ-200.

This international collaborative program is in considerable contrast to Western Europe's other major fighter project underway, the French Dassault-Breguet Rafale program. Rafale has, from the start, been an individual program pursued by the French, who traditionally work alone on military projects and are willing to pay the high costs of this approach. As a result, the French have a high percentage of capable, home-produced front line military equipment.

Both the production Rafale and the EFA will be developed primarily to meet the requirements identified by their respective countries of origin. The EFA program is aimed at meeting the relevant specific joint future fighter demands of all four Eurofighter member countries. It also presents the possibility of producing a level of standardization within four major Western European air arms. The costs involved in creating the new aircraft are shared between the member countries, precluding the need for a single country to develop its own fighter. However, a fully collaborative project has potential pitfalls. Among these are the need to harmonize national interests and requirements, and smooth out potential arguments and objections from various participants.

As a result of a process that lasted several years, the part-

ners in Eurofighter finally identified and agreed upon common needs for an agile, air-to-air combat fighter. A full project definition phase was ultimately launched which was completed in September 1986. The EFA will be designed to meet the European Staff Requirement agreed to during December 1985 and amplified in 1987.

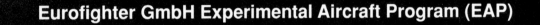

Eurofighter GmbH Experimental Aircraft Program (EAP)

It will be expected to fulfill a secondary role of air-to-ground attack missions in addition to its main task of air-to-air combat.

The Rafale program originated as the ACX (Avion de Combat Experimental) early in the 1980s, following preliminary studies which commenced in the late 1970s. During the ACX project the French were set to become fully involved as a member of the EFA program, but subsequently withdrew from this venture in 1985.

The production Rafale is intended to fulfill two separate requirements. These are the French Air Force's Avion de Combat Tactique (ACT) and the French Navy's Avion de Combat Marine (ACM) projects. The Air Force's tactical combat aircraft is planned to have air-to-air as well as air-to-ground capability. The French Navy Rafale (sometimes referred to as the Rafale M) will be capable of operating from aircraft carriers and will replace the French Navy's aging Vought F-8 Crusader fighters.

A common feature of the Rafale and EFA programs is the

45

large amount of new technology that will be included in the production aircraft. To this end, both projects are already employing a technology demonstrator in which many of the new concepts and materials to be used in the production aircraft are being thoroughly explored and tested.

The French Rafale A technology demonstrator first flew on July 4, 1986, exceeding Mach 1.3. It was maneuvered up to 5 Gs during this initial flight. In a successful test program this single aircraft has explored the Rafale's flight envelope, reaching a top speed of approximately Mach 2 and flying at well over 40,000 feet and up to 9 Gs. Of special significance have been the simulated deck landing trials using suitable facilities ashore in addition to actual approaches made at the French aircraft carriers Foch and Clemenceau. Although the Rafale A cannot perform an arrested landing aboard an aircraft carrier, these tests are fully relevant to the planned French Navy-operated production Rafale. The single Rafale A demonstrator is powered by two General Electric F404-GE-400 turbofan engines, each rated at approximately 16,000-lbs with afterburner.

The Eurofighter program's technology demonstrator, the Experimental Aircraft Program (EAP), has also proven of great value and is exploring many aspects which will be incorporated in the production EFA. However, like the Rafale A demonstrator, the single EAP does not represent a production standard. The EAP first flew on August 8, 1986, several weeks after the Rafale A, and exceeded Mach 1.1 on this flight.

The purpose of this aircraft, built by British Aerospace in collaboration with a number of industrial partner companies, is to demonstrate advanced tech-

nologies for next generation fighters. Like the Rafale A demonstrator, it makes use of new materials, improved aerodynamics, an advanced electronic cockpit, and a fly-by-wire flight control system. It is powered by two Turbo-Union RB.199 Mk.104D turbofan engines, each rated at nearly 16,000-lbs with afterburner.

The construction of eight EFA prototypes, including two two-seat aircraft, is planned. The first prototype is expected to fly in 1991. The third prototype powerplant will revert to the Eurojet EJ-200 engines, rated at 20,000-lbs with afterburner. Series production of the EFA could begin about 1993, with a proposed service entry of mid-1996.

The production EFA will weigh some 9.75 tons dry, with a wingspan of just under 34 feet 6 inches, and an overall length of approximately 48 feet. A large percentage of composite materials, including carbon fiber and aluminum-lithium, will be used. The cockpit will consist of state-of-the-art avionics equipment, with various multi-function color displays, and all will be integrated with the aircraft's flight control system through a NATO-standard databus. Pilot workload will be reduced where possible.

The EFA's delta wing will feature leading edge slats and trailing edge flaperons. Canard foreplanes will be mounted on each side of the cockpit. This "tail-less" canard delta layout,

with its various high-lift devices, plus the full-authority active control technology fly-by-wire flight control system, is planned to give the aircraft considerable agility and maneuverability, allowing "carefree" handling within the aircraft's own flying limits. The EFA will thus have the potential to become an excellent dogfighter. It will also have considerable Short Take Off and Landing (STOL) capability.

Armament will comprise an internal cannon, plus the ability to carry a mix of AIM-120 AMRAAM medium-range and AIM-132 ASRAAM or AIM-9 SIDE-WINDER short-range air-to-air missiles (AAMs). Four AMRAAMs will be carried semi-recessed beneath the fuselage/air intakes, with the short-range missiles on underwing pylons. A total of 15 external attachment points/pylons will allow a variety of air-to-ground weapons and stores to be carried. Maximum speed will be approximately Mach 1.8 to Mach 2, with an estimated combat radius of 350 miles.

In its production Rafale D form, France's independent fighter will also have very useful capabilities. The production Rafale will outwardly resemble the single Rafale A demonstrator. Five Rafale D/M prototypes are planned, a French government contract for these aircraft having been awarded to Dassault-Breguet in April 1988. The first flight is intended for 1990, with possible service entry in 1996.

Rafale A Capabilities Demonstrator

At 8.5 tons empty, the production Rafale will be about one ton lighter than the present Rafale A, and will be dimensionally smaller. Wingspan (over the wingtip-carried missiles) will be marginally over 35 feet, with a planned length of approximately 46 feet 7 inches. Like the EFA, it will comprise a high percentage of advanced materials in its airframe, and will feature a state-of-the-art cockpit. A Crouzet voice alarm warning system and voice command system are possible inclusions. This innovative equipment will give verbal information to the pilot and allow him to convey verbal commands to the aircraft for such planned functions as navigation, communications and weapons selection.

Like the EFA, the production Rafale is a "tail-less" canard delta layout, albeit with a double delta wing planform which features leading edge slats and trailing edge elevons. The Rafale will be highly maneuverable, with a full fly-by-wire flight control system, and will feature useful STOL characteristics. Armament will comprise up to two internal cannons, with the capability of carrying wingtip-mounted Matra MAGIC 2 short-range AAMs. For medium-range work, the new Matra MICA AAM will be carried on four locations under the fuselage. Four more MICAs can be carried beneath the wings if required. There will be a total of 12 external attachment points for a wide variety of air-to-ground weapons to be carried. These could include the French nuclear-capable ASMP missile.

The Rafale M will differ from the Rafale D in having a modified and strengthened landing gear and an arrestor hook for aircraft carrier operations. SNECMA's M88 turbofan engine, which will power the production Rafales, will possibly first fly in the Rafale A demonstrator during 1990. The 16,840-lbs with afterburner engine gives the twin-engined production Rafale a potential top speed of Mach 2.

The French requirement for production Rafales is likely to include approximately 300 aircraft, although a definite total has not yet been announced. The length of time envisaged before the type enters service, however, has presented a challenge to the French Navy, which has an increasingly pressing need for an F-8 Crusader replacement. This has resulted in the McDonnell Douglas F/A-18 Hornet being considered as an alternative to the Rafale M, although the arguments for the Rafale program could make this option moot.

The requirement for the production EFA runs to approximately 800 aircraft for the four participating countries, giving this particular project a major boost.

Both Dassault-Breguet and the Eurofighter consortium will actively search for export orders for their respective production aircraft, although the fighter market in the 1990s is likely to be as fiercely competitive as ever. In this sense the Rafale and EFA will be in competition not only with each other for potential export sales, but also will have to face major challenges from elsewhere. These include competition from United States-produced fighters, among them the future Advanced Tactical Fighter.

Both the Rafale and the EFA programs have yet to decide upon such important matters as the radar to be fitted in production-standard aircraft.

Nevertheless, despite the potential difficulties of fighter design, both projects appear set to develop impressive combat aircraft. [IDA]

Artist's concept of the new European Fighter Aircraft (EFA).

RAFALE RADAR

"Enhanced Multifunctionality"

by Gary L. Kieffer

Mr. Jean Pierre Chevenement, with the French Ministry of Defense, announced on December 7th, that Thomson-CSF and Electronique Serge Dassault (ESD) were directed to form a joint venture, led by Thomson-CSF, to manage the program of the ACT-ACM (avion de combat tactique-avion de combat marine) Rafale radar.

Within two months, the joint venture company is to present a proposal based on the general architecture of the Thomson-CSF's RDX E 2, but incorporating certain features of the ESD radar design. For the duration of the program, the work-sharing will be two-thirds for Thomson-CSF.

The Rafale radar will be multi-functional, able to accomplish air-to-air, air-to-ground and air-to-surface missions in all weather conditions, during daylight or night-time operations and in dense electronic warfare environments. The radar will offer terrain-following and avoidance at high speed, low level penetration.

On air-to-air missions, Rafale radar capabilities include the detection of approaching hostile targets at all altitudes within a range of more than 100 km, and constant contact throughout interception and combat phases. This is irrespective of the relative altitudes and directions of the targets and friendly fighter planes. Automatic target tracking, detailed analysis of adversaries, vital information for preparation of engagements, and the simultaneous engagement of eight separate targets using

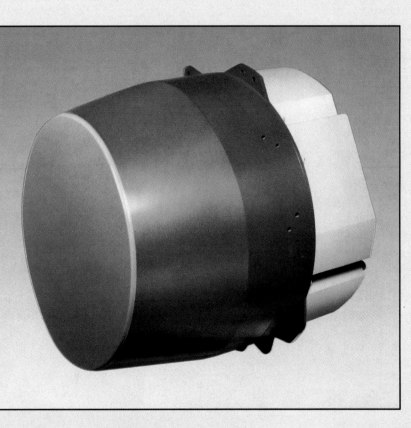

AMRAAM/MICA missiles are additional capabilities.

The Rafale radar design breaks new ground with its "enhanced multifunctionality," which interlaces air-to-air and air-to-ground modes to detect airborne targets while the aircraft is in very low level flight. Further, it can perform standoff detection of surface targets and fire control of air-to-surface missiles. Design features include passive, dual-axis electronic-scanning using the Thomson-CSF Radant process, which offers scanning agility with low sidelobes.

Thomson-CSF is also examining the integration of the radar with the navigation and weapons systems. This will help to maximize cooperation between the radar and the electro-optic sensors and ECM (electronic countermeasures) system.

The multi-function radar for the Rafale is designed to occupy a smaller volume and weigh considerably less than current designs, yet deliver power equivalent to present radars. The power consumption and weight reduction will be accomplished by using microelectronics, large scale hybrid circuits and monolithic integrated circuits.

New systems must be easy to use and the pilot's reaction time must be cut to a minimum to be effective. With the design for the ATF/Rafale radar, tremendous strides have been made by each of the manufacturers to produce a radar with great potential to fulfill both these requirements. IDA

MATRA MICA

AIMED FOR THE 90s
by Susan Malinowski-Turner

In keeping with the tradition of French weapon systems for use by French forces, MATRA DEFENSE has announced the full-scale development of the MICA (Interception, Combat and Self-defense Missile) missile, designed to fulfill the requirements of the French Air Force and Navy.

Using expertise gained from previously developed missiles and the requirements set forth by France's General Staff, MATRA MICA will utilize the latest in miniturization techniques to provide the air forces with a light multi-target missile.

Capable of carrying out long-distance interception, dogfight and self-defense missions, MICA will be fitted interchangeably with either an active radar or passive infrared homing head. Either seeker system can be used for all roles, making effective counter-measures against MICA an extremely difficult proposition.

MICA promises to provide a very effective defense against numerous opponents. The flight-tested jet-deflector system will allow considerable maneuvering capabilities under high load factors, enabling MICA to lock on to highly maneuverable targets. A multi-target capability allows simultaneous firing of several missiles directed at varying targets.

Three operating modes are available: long-range interception, medium-range interception and dogfight combat. Long-range interception involves inertial guidance plus mid-course trajectory updating and infrared homing head or active radar for terminal guidance. Inertial guidance and

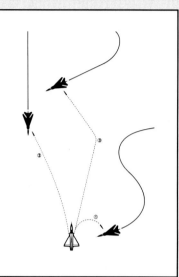

tracking by homing head for terminal phase is utilized for medium -range interception, with the missile having "fire-and-forget" capability, being fully self-sufficient after firing. For dogfight combat, MICA homing head locks on the target with active radar or infrared before or after firing. From lock on, the missile is "fire-and-forget."

The development phase for MATRA MICA commenced in April 1987, following numerous preliminary studies. It is expected to be operational as a main weapon system for future fighters or up-dated current fighters by 1993. IDA

RAFALE equipped with 4 MATRA MICA and 2 MAGIC missiles.

ELECTRIC JETS

by Damian Housman

Model of the F-16 Agile Falcon.

For the last 10 years, the General Dynamics/U.S. Air Force (USAF) F-16 Fighting Falcon has been among the world's premier fighter-bombers. Rather than rest on its successful design, which won the competition for the USAF contract in 1975, the F-16 has evolved over time into an even more effective combat aircraft. That evolution appears ready to continue well into the nineties.

Military hardware rarely remains the same. Improvements in threat systems, together with greater user experience and advancing technology, compel nearly all military hardware to improve with time. The F-16 is a good example of an aircraft that started out as the best all-around fighter, but which has undergone significant improvements over the years.

The F-16A (and its two-seat fighter trainer version, the F-16B) has been and continues to be the first line fighter of the United States and more than a dozen other countries. At combat weight (half internal fuel plus missiles), the Fighting Falcon could sustain a 9 G turn, and had a thrust-to-weight ratio better than 1:1. With modern radar, head-up display (HUD), fly-by-wire flight control system, and extremely precise bombing capability, the F-16 was everything a fighter pilot or air force could want — almost.

As users gained experience with their new aircraft, more capabilities were sought. This was not done in a scattergun approach, but in a deliberate program to incorporate improvements in a coherent, methodical way. The original F-16A Block 1 aircraft were enhanced to Block 5 and then Block 10 and 15 configuration. The horizontal tail area was increased, the 9 G capability was expanded from 22,500 lbs gross weight to 24,500 lbs, maximum takeoff weight was increased by 2,400 lbs, electrical cooling and wiring were improved, and other avionics enhancements were made.

The tremendous sales success of the F-16A brought about an unusual turn of events recently. The U.S. and international customers of the fighter have seen the introduction of a completely new version, the F-16C (and two-seat D). The quest for better capability from the A model has culminated in a massive upgrade. Block 10 and 15 aircraft are being raised to a new standard via the Operational Capability Upgrade (OCU). The OCU, which will apply to more than 1,400 production line and retrofit aircraft, will mean that F-16A users will continue to outperform possible competitors.

OCU enhancements include an expanded stores management computer, CARA radar altimeter, radar upgrades, AMRAAM provisions, a cockpit data transfer unit, an expanded fire control computer, and Penguin antishipping missile provisions. Takeoff gross weight will be increased to 37,500 lbs. The OCU upgrade will apply to approxi-

A four-ship formation of F-16As from the South Carolina National Guard.

First F-16A firing of AIM-7 SPARROW missile.

mately 139 production aircraft, and 1,278 retrofit aircraft. It should be completed by 1994.

An F-16A test airplane fired an AIM-7 for the first time in October 1988 at Edwards AFB, California. The F-16A Air Defense Fighter retrofit program will add AIM-7 SPARROW BVR missile capability to the F-16.

The AIM-7 capability will be particularly welcome news for pilots, who have wanted a beyond-visual-range (BVR) capability since the F-16 was first built. General Dynamics has always built the F-16 with BVR missiles in mind, though that option was not initially accepted by the USAF. This was less an operational than a political decision, made in the fear that Congress would see the F-16 as an alternative to the F-15, and kill the latter program. In any case, the USAF is now anxious to give the F-16 a BVR capability.

During the early 1980s, backers of the Northrop F-20 Tigershark had been pressing for sales of that fighter, both at home and abroad. But, the F-20 was designed in accordance with Carter Administration guidelines for an export fighter for Third World countries. Though technologically advanced, the F-20 lacked the range and weapon carrying capability of its U.S and international rivals. Thanks to the machinations of the "defense reformers" and their friends in Congress, there was a great hue and cry supporting the Tigershark as the fighter the Pentagon refused to buy despite

its low cost, ease of maintenance, and combat effectiveness. The ADF competition results, however, proved that the F-16 was superior to the F-20 in all categories.

The 270 F-16 air defense fighters going to USAF air defense units will not be newly procured. They will be modified F-16A aircraft already in the inventory. Each will go through the OCU upgrade. Then they will have modification performed by the Ogden (Utah) Air Logistics Center. The first of these modified Block 15 planes will be sent through Ogden in January 1989.

The air defense modifications will include several changes to the radar, to make it capable of detecting smaller targets, such as cruise missiles. It will also support the AIM-7 Sparrow and AIM-120 AMRAAM (Advanced Medium Range Air To Air Missile) radar guided missiles. Communications upgrades include the Have Quick II jam-resistant radio, and a long range HF radio. Provisions for a global positioning system (GPS) that would help keep track of position while out of range of ground navaids are also included in the modification. An IFF interrogator will help determine the identity of target aircraft. For visual identification of targets at night, a powerful light can be used to provide a better look.

All aircraft go through major changes every several years, and the F-16 has planned its modernization from the start. This plan, the Multinational Staged Improvement Plan (MSIP), has been

available to foreign operators of the F-16 as it has been for the USAF.

The first stage of the MSIP applied to the F-16A, beginning at production Block 15, includes provisions for the enhancements described above. The second stage began with production of Block 25, otherwise known as the F-16C, together with the two-seat D.

Changes to equipment and capability are enormous at Block 25. They include replacement of the APG-66 radar with the Westinghouse APG-68, advanced avionics and cockpit, a wider HUD than in the A model, better electrical and environmental systems, and the ability to fire AGM-65D imaging infrared MAVERICK air-to-surface missiles.

Additional changes in the engine inlet duct and common configured engine bay, made to accommodate both the F-100-PW-220 and F110-GE-100 (with nearly 29,000 lbs of thrust) engines, plus a full-up AMRAAM capability and ECM additions for survivability, have characterized Block 30 and 32 F-16C/D aircraft. The difference between them is that Block 30 uses the General Electric F110-GE-200 engine, while the Block 32 uses the Pratt & Whitney F100-PW-220.

One significant change to the radar allows it to track-while-scan as many as 10 targets simultaneously, much like the F-18. There is also a selectable ground moving target rejection function, velocity search, and raid cluster resolution for air-to-air.

Block 25 began production in 1984, with Block 30/32 in 1986. However, with many radar and avionics-related improvements largely software-related, it is not unusual to see Block 25 aircraft with Block 30 capabilities. One of the remarkable facets of the F-16 program is how rapidly improvements are made to prior production aircraft. In many cases it is a simple matter of playing a new software tape in an existing avionics computer. The F-16 is far less reliant on hardware changes than previous aircraft.

With the new radar, wiring for AMRAAM, increased takeoff weight (to 37,500 lbs), and expanded 9 G envelope, the F-16 was picking up capabilities not dreamed of by the designers of the original lightweight fighter in the early 1970s. It was also picking up additional weight, which has negatively influenced performance. For instance, at combat weight and at 10,000 feet altitude, a Block 30 aircraft will have five percent less instantaneous turn capability than the original production F-16A, and about 10 percent less sustained turn capability.

That has required serious thinking for fighter force planners. With more capability coming (Block 40/42 begins production deliveries in December 1989), the weight will continue to climb. As it does, performance will continue to suffer. Several elements are merging to regain the maneuverability edge the F-16 has had since the beginning.

Block 40/42 aircraft will feature a digital flight control computer and will have the same leading edge flap scheduling as the F-16A/B, which will improve aircraft maneuverability despite the additional weight of integrated electronic warfare equipment, LANTIRN night low-level attack provisions, accuracy enhancements, and advanced air-to-air IFF and missiles. Block 42 aircraft are only 13 percent less maneuverable than Block 10, and the GE-powered Block 40 is only five percent less maneuverable.

Block 50/52 aircraft, which will be out in 1991, will see the introduction not only of new combat capabilities, but also new engines. With an

internal self protection jammer, advanced radar warning receiver, advanced chaff/flare dispensers, fully integrated HARM and SHRIKE anti-radar missile capability, and other electronic changes, the F-16C will evolve to the limit. Both General Electric and Pratt & Whitney will produce a model of the increased performance engine (IPE),

a 29,000-lb class engine with a 20-30 percent increase in thrust. Maneuver performance will remain within five percent of Block 10 F-16A sustained turn rates. Another leap in maneuver capability will follow in the mid-1990s when Agile Falcon takes to the skies. There are, however, other aspects to the F-16 story which come first.

Characteristics

Wing Area . . . . 300 sq ft . . . . 27.9 sq m
Aspect Ratio . . . . 3.0 . . . . 3.0
Leading Edge Sweep . . . . 40º 40º
Weights:
  Empty (F100-PW-220 Engine) . . . 17,151 lb . . . . 7,780 Kg
  Empty (F110-GE-100 Engine) . . . . 17,933 lb . . . . 8,134 Kg
  Internal Fuel . . . . 6,972 lb . . . . 3,162 Kg
  Max TOGW . . . . 37,500 lb . . . . 17,010 Kg
Design Load Factor . . . . 9G 9G
Service Life . . . . 8,000 hr . . . . . . 8,000 hr
Engine Thrust:
  (F100-PW-220) . . . . 23,770 lb . . . . 105.8 kN
  (F110-GE-100) . . . . 28,984 lb . . . . 128.9 kN

Wing Change Balances Future Versions

F-16 ELEMENT	IMPROVEMENT / EVOLUTION			
AVIONICS	F-16A/B ———— F-16A/B OCU ———— F-16A/B MLU			Continual Upgrade to Improve Operational Capability
	F-16C/D Block 25 → Block 30 → Block 40 → Block 50			
ENGINE	F100 PW ── Common Engine Bay/AFE ── IPE			
	-100 ─ F110-GE-100			
	-200 ─ F100-PW-220			
	• Thrust 24,000 lb ————————— 29,000 lb			
	• Durability 1,800 TAC Cycles ——— 4,000 TAC Cycles			
WEAPONS CARRIAGE	• Munitions/Carriage Added to List			No Aerodynamic Improvements to Balance Thrust, Avionics, and Weight Growth
	─ AMRAAM ─ HARM ─ AIM-7 ─ LANTIRN			
	• Hardpoint Capability Increased			
AIRFRAME	Structural Growth to Maintain 9-Gs and to Accommodate Systems			
	F-16A/B F-16C/D			
	Flight Design Wt 22,500 lb @ 9g ——— 29,250 lb @ 9g			
	Wt Empty 15,328 lb ——————— 19,790 lb			

U.S. Navy F-16N at Miramar Naval Air Station.

In June 1987, the U.S. Navy took delivery of its first F-16N adversary aircraft. A total of 26 of these modified aircraft, including 22 single-seaters and four two-seaters, are being used to emulate Soviet aircraft tactics and capabilities. Based at Naval Air Stations (NAS) Miramar, Key West, and Oceana, these special F-16s use the F-16C airframe, APG-66 radar from the F-16A, ALE-40 chaff/flare dispenser, the GE F-110 engine, a strengthened wing, and the ALR-69 radar warning receiver. Though the gun has been eliminated, they are equipped with the F-16's air combat maneuvering instrumentation system which allows the entire air battle to be replayed later to all participants from any angle or level of detail on the ground. Since the F-16N has been considerably lightened, and since it uses a more powerful engine than the original F-16A/B, it has an excellent thrust-to-weight ratio.

Japan has selected the F-16 as the basis for its advanced FS-X program. While details are incomplete, the program is likely to include between 130 and 170 aircraft, with a primary mission of sea-lane surveillance and antishipping. The prime contractor is Mitsubishi Heavy Industries of Japan, with General Dynamics as the main subcontractor. First flight is expected to take place in 1993, with deliveries commencing in 1997. The final configuration is yet to be selected; so it could differ considerably from any previous F-16.

The USAF has announced its intention of replacing the RF-4C tactical reconnaissance aircraft with a version of the F-16, the RF-16. Since there are internal space restrictions in the F-16 which preclude mounting recon systems inside the aircraft, it will require a pod. General Dynamics has been developing a pod recon system which incorporates near-real-time electro-optical sensor systems and recorded imaging systems. This allows rapid transmissions of time-sensitive intelligence and high resolution products that are used for detailed analysis. Final pod and sensor selection will depend on Air Force requirements. This version of the F-16 will be a single-seater.

The Air Force is looking at its options concerning close air support (CAS). A current agreement with the Army assigns the fixed wing CAS role to the Air Force. Presently assigned this mission, the A-10 is slow and unsurvivable in a high-threat environment. The Air Force wants a version of the F-16, tentatively called the A-16, to handle the mission, while certain OSD (Office of the Secretary of Defense) officials want other options explored, including a new, purpose-built plane.

The evolving A-16, if finally chosen, will handle the CAS

An F-16C equipped with MAVERICK air-to-surface missiles.

mission somewhat differently than present aircraft. It will be a techno-logical leap ahead. Target acquisi-tion can be autonomous, but also take advantage of scout helicopters through the Automatic Target Handoff System (ATHS), currently employed from Army OH-58D scout helicopters. The scout locates a target or group of targets, and automatically transmits target infor-mation to the A-16. A target cue is displayed on the A-16's HUD, showing the pilot where the target is located. The idea is to acquire and attack targets quickly and accu-rately, thus minimizing attrition.

Several night vision and naviga-tion systems are under considera-tion, including GEC's Atlantic FLIR pod, Martin Marietta's Pathfinder, the Hughes TINS, the Ford Nite Owl, and Texas Instruments' Falcon Eye. The pilot will also be aided by lightweight night vision goggles or, in the case of Falcon Eye, a helmet-mounted display and head-steered sensor. A highly effective auto-matic terrain following system developed by British Aerospace, called TERPROM, is a much touted candidate for inclusion. The system is relatively inexpensive, and uses only the radar altimeter as a sensor, in much the same way as the cruise missile determines position. Pilots report that TERPROM is in a class by itself for effectiveness.

F-16 Weapons Carriage Capability

M61 Gun & 511 Rds

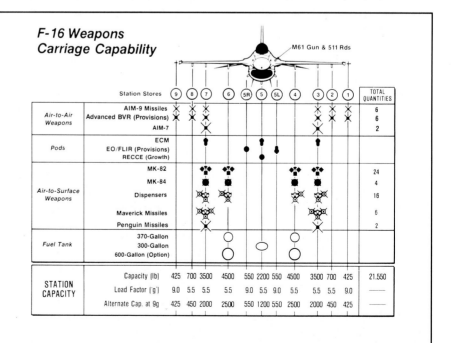

	Station Stores	9	8	7	6	5R	5	5L	4	3	2	1	TOTAL QUANTITIES
Air-to-Air Weapons	AIM-9 Missiles	X	X	X						X	X	X	6
	Advanced BVR (Provisions)	X	X	X						X	X	X	6
	AIM-7			X						X			2
Pods	ECM						X						
	EO/FLIR (Provisions)				X	X	X	X		X			
	RECCE (Growth)						X						
Air-to-Surface Weapons	MK-82		X	X						X	X		24
	MK-84			X		X				X			4
	Dispensers			X		X				X	X		16
	Maverick Missiles			X						X			6
	Penguin Missiles			X						X			2
Fuel Tank	370-Gallon				O				O				
	300-Gallon						O						
	600-Gallon (Option)				O				O				
STATION CAPACITY	Capacity (lb)	425	700	3500	4500	550	2200	550	4500	3500	700	425	21.550
	Load Factor ('g')	9.0	5.5	5.5	5.5	9.0	5.5	9.0	5.5	5.5	5.5	9.0	—
	Alternate Cap. at 9g	425	450	2000	2500	550	1200	550	2500	2000	450	425	—

The Agile Falcon is designed to complement the Advanced Tactical Fighter.

The next major evolutionary Fighting Falcon will probably be a multi-national design and production effort, with the first aircraft availability around 1995. The Agile Falcon is conceived as a complement to the Advanced Tactical Fighter (ATF), much as the F-16 is a complement to the F-15. Our international F-16 partners have been invited to take part in the design and production of the Agile Falcon.

The proposed Agile Falcon will combine several structural upgrades with what is now conceived as Block 50 avionics. Tentatively referred to as Block 60, the Agile Falcon will have a wing area 30 percent larger than the F-16C, allowing better turn and cruise performance. The increased performance engine, with 29,000 lbs of thrust in full afterburner, will also contribute to higher thrust-to-weight ratios and better turning capability.

Agile Falcon will regain the maneuverability of the F-16A, with all the advanced systems capability of the F-16C plus additional payload capability. With today's highly

effective point-and-shoot weapons such as the AIM-9L/M SIDE-WINDER, the aircraft with the first shot after the merge will get the kill. If we assume two aircraft, the Agile Falcon and the generic advanced threat aircraft of the 1990s, 180 degrees out at the encounter, the maneuverability of Agile Falcon to point its nose at the threat before the threat does the same gives it a decided advantage.

Yet to be determined is the final configuration. Although the structure of all Agile Falcons will be essentially the same, the European partners have an all-F-16A/B fleet, while the U.S. has a mixed F-16A/B/C/D fleet. Many additional avionics choices are available, such as TERPROM, internal ECM suites, radar warning receivers, a developmental infrared search and track (IRST) system, etc. The flexibility of the Fighting Falcon in utilizing a vast array of combat systems is well established. A related program is the F-16A/B mid-life update, which would use some of the new avionics of the Agile Falcon.

So it appears that the evolutionary Fighting Falcon will continue to play a pivotal role in the defense of Western-allied nations for the foreseeable future. With at least 18 nations operating or committed to buying the F-16, and with more than 4,000 acquired or planned to date worldwide, the "electric jet" has been firmly established as one of the best all-around fighters of all time. IDA

Damian Housman is currently working on his book ELECTRIC JET — THE STORY OF THE F-16 FIGHTING FALCON, to be published in 1989 by Arms and Armour Press of London. This is intended to be the definitive work on the F-16. Mr. Housman is a military affairs writer and public relations professional residing in the Washington area. He is also a Weapon Systems Officer in the F-4D Phantom II fighter-bomber, with the 121st Tactical Fighter Squadron, District of Columbia Air National Guard.

AMRAAM

Advanced Medium-Range Air-to-Air Missile

by J. Philip Geddes

No matter how fast or agile a fighter aircraft may be, its ultimate effectiveness depends on its weapons. Air combat has been waiting for decades for an all-weather missile that could launch and leave, fly faster, resist countermeasures, be easy to maintain, and small enough to be carried in multiples. The "wish list" missile to replace the AIM-7 SPARROW also had to fit the best fighters in the West and those yet to be built. That medium-range missile, developed by Hughes Aircraft Company, has finally arrived at the end of a seven-year development program.

In the course of development, the program was attacked over and over again as being too ambitious and too costly, with detractors claiming the end product would not be worth the price. Every failure was pounced on as evidence for the negative point of view. They were wrong. Advanced Medium-Range Air-to-Air Missile (AMRAAM) works and is entering a shared production program that will run well into the next century.

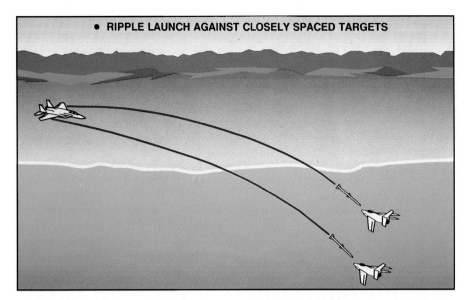

● RIPPLE LAUNCH AGAINST CLOSELY SPACED TARGETS

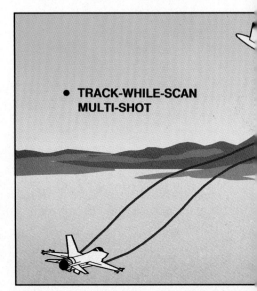

● LONG RANGE TWS DUAL LAUNCH

AMRAAM is a fairly small 7-inch (in) diameter, 12-foot (ft) long missile weighing 345 pounds (lbs), guided by a state-of-the-art active radar seeker, which allows a pilot to ripple fire several missiles at a like number of targets and maneuver out of danger while the missiles guide themselves to the individual targets. Bad weather won't stop AMRAAM. Maneuvering into position for launch is easier for the pilot than with today's missiles because of the wide launch envelope. Targets can be "beyond visual range", out of sight over 30 miles away.

Hughes Aircraft Missile Systems Group delivered the first production AMRAAM in September 1988 but waited another month to officially roll out in full ceremony. Hughes Aircraft Co. Chairman Dr. Malcom R. Currie said at the roll-out that AMRAAM was one of the finest

achievements in the history of his company. The first USAF unit to receive AMRAAM will be the 33rd Tactical Fighter Wing, based at Eglin Air Force Base (AFB), Florida. Initial Operating Capability (IOC) is set for the Fall of 1989.

PUSHING THE LIMITS

At the roll-out ceremony for the first missile, Brigadier General Charles E. Franklin, Director of the AMRAAM Joint Systems Program Office, gave some measure of the design achievement. He stated that the designers took the three-foot diameter, 500-lb radar from the F-15 and shrunk it to six inches in diameter and 90 lbs in weight. This package, he noted, flies several times farther than the best missile the Air Force has today, 50 percent faster and with a 30 percent reduction in weight. General Franklin said AMRAAM introduces

a new era in air-to-air combat for the Air Force, Navy, and our allies, providing a true force-multiplier that enables pilots to fight numerically superior forces and come away winners. He observed that the political environment during development was often as difficult as the technical, with constant oversight, crises and second guessing. He added that there is still a perception of uncontrolled costs in the program, which overlooks the fact that the predictions of six years ago are within 0.2 percent of the first Selected Acquisition Review of 1982 - an accomplishment of which any venture would be proud.

SCORE CARD

As production deliveries began, AMRAAM had achieved a 78 percent success rate in 68 development guided firings from the F-14, F-15, F-16 and F/A-18. A closer

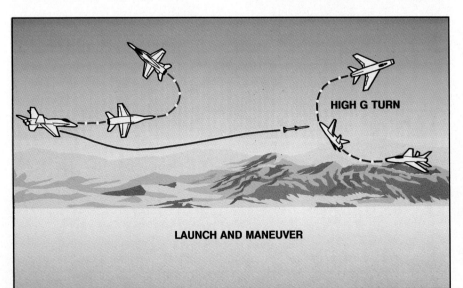

HIGH G TURN

LAUNCH AND MANEUVER

● TRACK-WHILE-SCAN MULTI-SHOT

● SHOOT DOWN AGAINST CLUSTER
IN AN ECM ENVIRONMENT

look at the live firings shows 58 successful including 18 direct hits — missiles passing within lethal range of the warhead are successes — with only 15 failures. The fact that any missiles should fail in a development program seemed to baffle some critics. After the current series of tests with preproduction missiles are completed, there will be selective launches of up to 13 Lot I production units as needed.

PRODUCTION SHARING

Lot I is the first production batch of AMRAAMs, derived from the full scale development contract awarded in December 1981. Lot I production is split between Hughes and second source Raytheon in a leader/follower arrangement with Hughes building 105 and Raytheon 75. Raytheon will build 15 "qualifying missiles" in Lot 1, with deliveries starting in 1989, of which five will be

flight tested. The qualifying round is to ensure that the second source production meets the specification. Hughes will complete its last Lot I missile in August 1989.

Modest production in Lot II of 400 units is split with Hughes building 223 missiles and Raytheon 177. The Royal Air Force (RAF) in Britain plans to test 11 missiles from Lot II, with 10 instrumented and one captive. Lot III has been reduced to 900 missiles from 1,270 largely as a result of Congress cutting funds for the original higher quantities planned for Lots I and II. Planned production is still structured under former Secretary of Defense Weinberger's cost containment cap of 17,000 for the Air Force at a price of $5.2 billion in 1984 dollars spread over 11 years. Hughes Aircraft was forced to fund the final phase of development with an additional $250 million of its

own. The Navy plans to buy 7,320 missiles as part of a separate agreement for the F-18 and late model F-14Ds, bringing the total cost of the program to $7.585 billion in 1984 dollars.

Apart from Navy AMRAAM, Hughes and Raytheon are working in a joint venture known as H & R Company, in the competition to develop a long-range Advanced Air-to-Air Missile (AAAM) to replace the long-range (over 100-mile) PHOENIX missile for Navy fighters and Advanced Tactical Aircraft (ATA). PHOENIX is the primary weapon for the F-14 carrier-based fighter. The new missile will be compatible with the Air Force's Advanced Tactical Fighter (ATF) as well as Navy fighters. AAAM work is being performed under a $110 million 52-month contract, for which incremental funding began in September 1988.

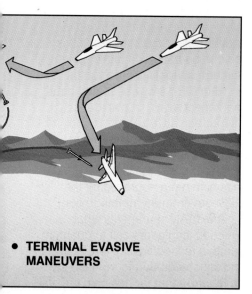

● TERMINAL EVASIVE
MANEUVERS

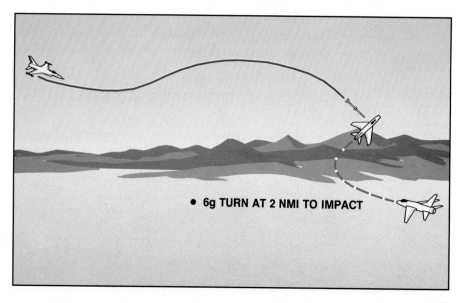

● 6g TURN AT 2 NMI TO IMPACT

AMRAAM OVERSEAS

European nations are interested in a dual production agreement to build AMRAAM, stemming from the 1980 Memorandum of Understanding (MoU) between the U.S., West Germany, and the United Kingdom (UK). Most offshore licensing agreements have traditionally followed much later in production between Lots VII to X. The first European produced AMRAAMs would probably be in the Lot IV configuration. Looking ahead, the total market for AMRAAM in the U.S. and Europe alone could add up to at least 45,000 missiles. Other countries, including Japan, Australia and Canada have shown interest in buying the missile.

After months of difficult negotiations, at the time of writing, there had been little movement on both sides to accommodate a program on how to build AMRAAM in Europe. EURAAM, the joint venture between MBB and AEG in West Germany and BAe and Marconi in the UK had difficulty in accepting the opening terms of a coproduction program negotiated with AMRAAM International Licensing Company (AILC), a joint venture between Hughes and Raytheon.

Under the 1980 MoU, the European nations involved could coproduce or procure through the U.S. Foreign Military Sales program as desired.

Agreement, already hard to reach, was complicated by the transfer in mid-1988 of the lead position in the Advanced Short-Range Air-to-Air Missile (ASRAAM) SIDEWINDER replacement to the UK. This resulted in West Germany taking the lead in AMRAAM and reshuffling its AMRAAM contractors. Once West Germany has selected a prime contractor for AMRAAM, negotiations with AILC will likely reopen shortly thereafter.

The U.S. offer, announced in July 1988, to sell the UK 330 AMRAAMs for $157 million set a price comparison between a direct Foreign Military Sale (FMS) and coproduction. There have been accusations that the price for this batch was deliberately set too low for the coproducers to meet and thus force an FMS buy which is to the U.S.'s advantage.

The first requirement for AMRAAM in Europe is on the Sea Harrier, which the UK had left open as an optional FMS buy. Sea Harrier testing will begin with 11 test units that will come out of U.S. Lot

II, to be delivered to the UK in 1990. Whether the 330 missiles offered to the UK will be accepted for Sea Harrier depends on the results of the 11 tests. No particular problems are anticipated by Hughes with Sea Harrier, based on success in integrating the system on several U.S. fighters.

Production in Europe for the UK and West Germany, plus Norway at the 7,500-unit level being discussed, cannot compete with the economy of scale in the planned U.S. production of over 20,000 missiles. In short, European missiles will cost more. Hughes suggested European companies could join a "work sharing" program with AILC for subassemblies as an alternative to coproduction. Specific U.S. cost advantages in work sharing advanced by Hughes are in the areas of hybrid and large-scale integration electronic assemblies. A "co-assembly" program from this U.S. viewpoint would offer the lowest unit price with low risk. Over the long life expectancy for AMRAAM in the U.S., co-assembly could always grow into coproduction.

Should the UK and West Germany build AMRAAMs for other NATO countries, the 7,500-production-run would become much larger. Norway has already requested admittance to the AMRAAM production program in addition to its place in ASRAAM. Under the 1980 MoU, participating countries nominate aircraft for integrating AMRAAM. Studies have already begun on the Sea Harrier, Tornado, F4F, and the Mirage 2000. French interest in AMRAAM for the Mirage 2000 is said to be based on making that aircraft competitive against the F-16 and F-18 overseas and does not reflect a lack of confidence in Matra's MICA. Hughes and Dassault will conduct a similar study for the Rafale in the near future. The Swedish JAS39 Gripen has also been approved by the U.S. government for integration.

AMRAAM represents what Hughes' engineers call a "quantum jump in technology." There is every indication that daring from the start to leapfrog that far has paid off. IDA

Fighters Over Israel

by Lon Nordeen

During the past 42 years, the air arm of Israel has developed from a collection of war surplus light planes into a first class Air Force with a battle proven reputation. Since 1947, the Israeli Air Force (IAF) has participated in five major wars, several small scale conflicts, hundreds of border confrontations, and clashes with terrorists. In the course of these actions IAF aircrews have destroyed more than 1,200 aircraft, over 700 in air combat, and have flown hundreds of thousands of attack and support sorties.

Israel has relied on its air arm, its reserve army, and small navy for defense against the military forces of neighboring countries. Israel's adversaries have continuously received advanced aircraft and other military systems from the Soviet Union and Western suppliers. Surrounded by and faced with numerically superior enemies, Israel has generally taken an aggressive stance. The IAF has usually served as the spear point. Israeli pilots, flying French, Israeli or American-built aircraft, have faced off against and bested first line Soviet planes and air defense weapons. Repeated conflicts and the necessity to prepare for war on a daily basis have given the IAF an operational heritage which no other Air Force can match.

The IAF can trace its history to November 10, 1947 when an air service, with a total strength of 11 light planes, was organized. With the establishment of the State of Israel on May 14, 1948, full scale war broke out. Israel's force of light planes bombed attacking Arab columns. But, they could not contest the Egyptian fighters and bombers which repeatedly attacked Tel Aviv and other cities.

Since well before the outbreak of the War of Independence, Israeli agents were working to acquire aircraft and weapons and to enlist volunteers to man its fledgling air arm. One of the most important early acquisitions was a small number of C-46 and C-47 transports which were smuggled out of the United States.

The 1948 Israeli Avia, a copy of the German Messerschmitt Bf-109G.

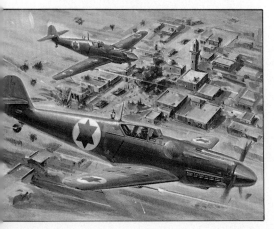

During the latter part of May 1948, these transports flew almost nonstop between Czechoslovakia and Israel carrying rifles, machine guns, ammunition and disassembled Avia fighter planes. Israel's first fighter plane, the Avia, was a copy of the German Messerschmitt Bf-109G which was built in Czechoslovakia. On their first mission, flown on May 29, 1948, IAF Avia pilots attacked and halted an Egyptian column advancing toward Tel Aviv. Five days later Modi Allon, Commander of 101 Squadron, the first IAF fighter unit, shot down two Egyptian Dakotas over Tel Aviv.

Israel was able to acquire a wide variety of aircraft, including Spitfires, Mustangs, B-17s, and Dakotas, and attracted large numbers of foreign volunteers. A majority of the volunteers came from the United States, Canada, England, and South Africa. As a result, English became the primary language of the IAF during the War of Independence. The IAF supported the ground war with many attack and transport missions, and downed over 20 enemy aircraft in air combat.

After the War of Independence, the volunteers went home. The IAF then set out to train an all Israeli force and rationalize its inventory of aircraft. Because of budgetary limitations and political restrictions, the air arm concentrated on buying surplus Spitfires, Mustangs, Mosquitoes and C-47 transports from a variety of European countries.

Air battles in the Korean skies during the early 1950s demonstrated that piston-engined fighters were no match for the new jets. To counter the threat of Arab jet fighters, the IAF joined the jet age in 1953 by purchasing a squadron of Meteor fighters from England. In 1955, Egypt signed a friendship pact with the Soviet Union and began a program to modernize the Egyptian armed forces. The arrival of large numbers of Soviet-built MiG-15 fighters and IL-28 bombers upset the air power balance in the Middle East.

Israel turned to France for support and purchased the Ouragon jet in 1955 and the Mystere IV fighter in 1956. The Mystere IV was the equal of the Soviet-built MiG-15, but Israel

could afford only a small quantity of these new fighters. Older Mustang, Mosquito and B-17 aircraft still accounted for almost half of the IAF tactical force. Conflict along the Israel/Egypt border gave the IAF the opportunity to demonstrate the effectiveness of these new jet fighters.

Following a period of tension, Israel went to war with Egypt in November 1956. The IAF flew air patrol, ground attack and support missions to assist Israeli ground forces. To the Air Force it was a frustrating conflict. In response to a request by Prime Minister David Ben Gurion, two French Air Force fighter squadrons defended Israeli air space from attack by Egyptian jet bombers. Also, British and French aircraft bombed the major military airfields in Egypt and effectively grounded the Egyptian Air Force. Air combat opportunities were few and far between and Mystere IV pilots only achieved seven victories. About a dozen IAF aircraft were lost, most falling to antiaircraft fire. Only one was a jet.

The successful use of battle tanks and aircraft in the 1956 conflict prompted Israel to expand and modernize these forces. The air arm in particular was given special emphasis because aircraft could defend Israel's skies and carry the fight to the enemy to buy time for the reserve ground forces to mobilize. Ezer Weizmen, who took command of the IAF soon after the 1956 conflict, fully embraced the new offensive doctrine. He stated that, "Israel's best defense is in the skies over Cairo."

Israel continued its good relationship with France and the IAF became a prime customer of French fighter aircraft. The IAF's piston-engined planes were replaced by modern Mystere IV, Vautour, Super Mystere and Mirage III jets. Intense training and realistic exercises honed the IAF pilots, ground crews and all support personnel into an efficient fighting machine.

Violent incidents along the Syrian border increased in the mid-1960s and ultimately the IAF intervened. A number of dogfights took place and several Syrian MiG-21 fighters

The F-16 has proven itself in battle over Lebanon and is credited with over 40 air combat victories.

were shot down. On November 28, 1966 Israeli Mirages downed two Egyptian MiG-19 jets that were attempting to hit a Piper Cub scout plane over the Negev Desert. This dogfight saw the first successful use of air-to-air guided missiles in Middle East combat. One of the MiGs was hit and destroyed by a Matra 530 air-to-air missile. Tensions between Israel, Egypt and Syria increased, setting the stage for a war neither side wanted.

The highly successful Israeli preemptive airstrikes flown on June 5, 1967 had a major impact on the outcome of the conflict and established the reputation of the IAF. Israel took a calculated risk committing almost its entire inventory of fighters to attack Arab airfields. The gamble paid off. It was not an easy task. The Egyptians, Syrians and Jordanians fought back with determination. With air superiority attained, however, the IAF focused its attention on Arab ground forces to assist the Israeli Army. After six days, Israel had captured the Sinai Peninsula, Golan Heights, Jerusalem and

Jordan's West Bank Territory. The IAF had shot down 60 Arab aircraft in air combat and destroyed 380 on the ground, but lost 46 planes and 24 pilots. Following the 1967 War, Egypt, Syria, and Jordan rapidly rebuilt their armed forces and various terrorist groups initiated a harassment campaign against Israel.

The close relationship between Israel and France ended in 1967 because of Charles de Gaulle's arms embargo. The United States had agreed to supply Israel with 48 A-4 Skyhawk fighter-bombers in 1966 .These were delivered in 1968. While these planes made up for the losses experienced in the Six-Day War, the IAF needed a new supply of supersonic fighters. Denied the Mirage V, Israel set out to produce a copy of this aircraft. After lengthy negotiations, Israel obtained the approval to purchase two squadrons of F-4 Phantoms.

In 1969, President Nasser of Egypt declared a War of Attrition against Israel. With artillery barrages, commando raids and air strikes, Egypt continuously struck

at the Israelis. Mounting casualties prompted Israel to hit back with heavy air strikes. Repeated terrorist assaults and artillery fire broke the calm along the Syrian and Jordanian borders. IAF fighter-bombers, including the new Skyhawks, blasted terrorist bases in retaliation.

Along the Suez Canal, fighting intensified. Both sides introduced new weapons; Israel now had the F-4 Phantom and, with Soviet assistance, Egypt built up a massive air defense network of interlocking anti-aircraft missiles and guns. In January 1970, the IAF began to fly raids against targets near Cairo. This prompted the Soviet Union to deploy fighters and missile crews to defend Egyptian airspace.

Due to Soviet intervention, the IAF ended its deep penetration bombing but blasted the expanding air defenses near the Suez Canal and shot down many Egyptian planes. With Soviet pilots flying patrol missions, a clash was inevitable.

On July 30, 1970 IAF Phantoms and Mirages fought with Soviet fighters. Five MiG-21s were shot down. A cease-fire was called on August 8, 1970, ending the fighting. The IAF dealt severe blows to the terrorists and shot down 113 Arab and Soviet planes. Soviet supplied missiles and guns, however, had exacted a toll of 26 IAF planes and many pilots.

In the early 1970s, the IAF received numerous new Skyhawks, Phantoms and home-built Nesher fighters. During this period, the IAF frequently bombed terrorist camps and fought several aerial engagements with Syrian planes.

The simultaneous attack by Egypt and Syria on October 6, 1973 caught Israel by surprise. The IAF went into immediate action. Egyptian fighter-bombers hit Israeli headquarters, airfields and Hawk missile sites in the Sinai. Defending Israeli fighter and antiaircraft units man-

aged to shoot down about a dozen of the Arab planes in the first wave of attackers. An IAF Mirage also intercepted and destroyed a KELT air-to-surface missile heading toward Tel Aviv.

IAF fighter-bombers swooped in to attack and met a withering barrage of missile and gun fire. Egypt had upgraded its air defense. Syria deployed a similar network which included many new Soviet-supplied weapons like the mobile SA-6 SAM, the shoulder-fired SA-7 SAM and ZSU-23 four-barrel cannon. Fighter pilots were capable of evading several missiles; but when faced with dozens of missiles and massed gunfire, they were overwhelmed. Over 50 IAF aircraft were lost during the first three days of the conflict.

Once the situation on the ground was stabilized, the IAF began to con-

centrate more on hitting targets like airfields, convoys and headquarters well behind the battle zone. New tactics, electronic countermeasures (ECM) systems and better coordination reduced the IAF loss rate to ground support missiles over the battlefield.

Fighter pilots flew almost non-stop to the point that their oxygen masks ripped into their faces. Mirage and Phantom crews engaged in hundreds of dogfights, shooting down over 300 Arab aircraft during the 18-day conflict. Most of these victories were achieved with infrared homing air-to-air missiles such as the SIDE-WINDER and Israeli-built SHAFRIR. About a third fell to cannon fire. Anti-aircraft units downed 55 enemy aircraft with HAWK missiles and cannon fire, reflecting the high Arab ground attack effort.

When the cease-fire took effect on October 24, 1973, the Syrians had been pushed back from the Golan Heights and a significant portion of Egyptian territory was in Israeli hands. The IAF had flown over 12,000 sorties in 18 days and suffered 110 aircraft losses, most of which were hit by SAMs and gunfire. Over 200 IAF planes were damaged. Due to the massive American resupply effort, at the end of the war the IAF had about the same numerical strength as it did at the outset. Nevertheless, members of the air arm, like the Israeli population in general, were shocked by the war and the heavy losses suffered.

Following the war, the IAF examined the lessons of the conflict and concluded that improvements in training, intelligence collection and dissemination, tactics and weaponry

were needed. The antiaircraft branch was strengthened and liaison with ground troops improved to better plan the role and missions of air power. New aircraft, such as the Kfir, F-15 and AH-1 attack helicopters were ordered. Additional Phantoms and Skyhawks were received. To prevent a future surprise, assault intelligence collection platforms like the E-2C radar-warning aircraft, OV-1 Mohawk and RU-21 reconnaissance planes were placed into service. Many RPV programs were also started.

While peace talks between Israel and Egypt bore fruit, terrorist groups and Syria were increasing their attacks. In retaliation IAF fighter-bombers, including the new Kfir, routinely blasted terrorist bases in Lebanon. IAF C-130 transports made possible the highly publicized

F-4 Phantoms replaced earlier French aircraft during the late 1960s. These high-performance jets considerably upgraded the air combat and ground attack capabilities of the IAF.

Israeli F-15 pilots have shot down more than 50 Syrian aircraft over Lebanon and participated in long-range and attack missions.

Entebe rescue mission conducted in 1976. Israeli airpower supported Israeli ground troops during their 1978 invasion of Lebanon.

Israel viewed Syrian involvement in Lebanon as a threat. When MiGs began to interfere with IAF sorties, they were dealt with harshly. On June 27, 1979 five Syrian MiG 21s were shot down over Lebanon by IAF F-15s. Israeli attacks and air combat engagement continued. In April 1981, newly delivered F-16 fighters shot down two Mi-8 transport helicopters over Lebanon. As a result of this, Syria moved a large number of SAM batteries into Lebanon's Bekaa Valley. Israel protested the action and stepped up its air actions in Lebanon.

The IAF shocked the world with the successful raid against the Iraqi nuclear reactor near Baghdad. The long-range raid was performed in June 1981 by IAF pilots who flew the F-16 in the bombing role and the F-15 as an escort fighter.

Large scale fighting again erupted on June 6, 1982 when Israel invaded Lebanon to destroy terrorist bases. As tanks and infantry drove relentlessly north, IAF fighter-bombers and helicopter gunships blasted the defenders. Conflict with Syrian forces in Lebanon was inevitable. A full-scale attack on SAM batteries by the IAF in coordination with ground force artillery on June 9th destroyed most of the Syrian air defense shield in Lebanon. The Syrians threw in dozens of MiG-21 and -23 fighters in an attempt to thwart attacking Israeli planes. High-flying E-2C AWACS aircraft monitored their approach and vectored F-15s and F-16s to intercept. At the end of three days of intense air battles, more than 80 Syrian aircraft had been shot down and about 20 SAM batteries destroyed, for the loss of but one Israeli Skyhawk and three helicopters. Heavy air and ground action continued in Lebanon until August 1982 when the PLO and Syria agreed to pull their forces out of Beirut. Despite a cease-fire, air attacks and dogfights continued.

A PLO base almost 1,000 miles from Israel was bombed by the IAF in October 1985 and two Syrian MiG-23 fighters were shot down over Lebanon a month later.

In spite of the Syrian challenge, the IAF continued its reconnaissance and bombing attacks against suspected terrorist targets in Lebanon.

The IAF today includes about 450 F-15, F-16, F-4, Kfir and A-4 tactical aircraft plus hundreds of support systems ranging from advanced radar networks to trainers. All Mirage/Nesher fighters have been sold or retired and older A-4s moth-

balled or transferred to other countries. Many early model Kfir jets have been sold to Ecuador, Columbia and leased to the U.S. Navy and Marine Corps for use as adversary aircraft. The Fouga Magister is still the IAF's primary jet trainer. These planes were upgraded by Israel Aircraft Industries in the late 1970s.

The IAF surveillance network includes E-2C, 707, OV-1 Mohawk, Beech RU-21, and Westwind Sea Scan aircraft, numerous ground and balloon-mounted radars and a multitude of RPV drones. IAF 707 and C-130 aircraft serve in both refueling and transport roles while C-47s were gradually being phased out, being replaced by Israeli-built Arava aircraft. The helicopter component includes the CH-53D, SA-321, Bell 212, Bell 206B and other types. A small number of Aerospatiale HH-65A Dolphin helicopters serve with the Navy. The UH-60 Black Hawk was selected to

replace aging light and medium lift vehicles. The IAF attack helicopter force of AH-1 Cobras and Model 500 Defenders is being upgraded with new weapons and sensors.

As the 1980s draws to a close, the IAF faces a series of new challenges. The air arms of its potential opponents have been receiving an infusion of advanced aircraft. Syria has the Soviet-built MiG-29, Saudi Arabia the Tornado and the F-15 Eagle, while Jordan is buying the French Mirage 2000 and the Tornado. The qualitative improvement in Arab aircraft, weapons and pilot experience has diminished Israel's margin of air superiority.

The introduction of advanced short- and medium-range surface-to-surface missiles into the armed forces of Syria, Iraq and Saudi Arabia has created a new threat to Israel. The fighters and HAWK surface-to-air missiles of the IAF have almost no capability to intercept

these high-speed weapons. Modern Soviet and Chinese produced SS-12, SS-21 and CSS2 missiles, armed with conventional or chemical warheads, could damage Israeli airfields, hit army reserves and threaten civilian population centers. The Israeli military and civilian leadership has made it known that it will not tolerate an attack by surface-to-surface missiles and would retaliate with all means at its disposal. At the same time, Israel has initiated a sizable program to develop and field air defense missiles capable of shooting down tactical ballistic missiles.

The peace treaty with Egypt and budget cutbacks have had a significant impact on the IAF. In August 1987, the Israeli cabinet decided to cancel the Lavi fighter. IAF Kfirs, Skyhawks and other aircraft were grounded and training cut back in order to save money.

As the IAF moves into the 1990s,

quality rather than numbers will be in focus. In the wake of the Lavi cancellation, additional F-16s and F-15s were ordered. These new fighters will be supported by Phantoms, which are being upgraded in Israel, and declining numbers of Skyhawk and Kfir fighter-bombers. Advanced avionics and ECM systems developed for the Lavi are being fitted to IAF aircraft and new standoff weapons put into service. Intensified training and high standards ensure that all IAF personnel remain ready for action. This is vital because, with each passing year, combat-experienced pilots, maintenance personnel, ordnance handlers and other veterans retire from the force.

The IAF has a proud heritage. The force has defended the skies over Israel, achieved over a 25 to 1 victory-to-loss ratio in air combat and performed thousands of successful attack and reconnaissance sorties over hostile territory. Success has been achieved in the past due to training, motivation, good equipment and a willingness to do what is necessary to get the job done. Members of the Israeli Air Force — fighter pilots, mechanics and the troops who man air defense systems — know they are Israel's first line of defense. The safety of the country rests in their hands. IDA

Lon Nordeen (author) and Ken Kotik (artist/illustrator) collaborated to produce FIGHTERS OVER ISRAEL, the history of the Israeli Air Force. This new book, which includes 45 illustrations created especially for the project, 150 photographs and many first-person accounts of combat operations, will soon be released by Orion Books, a division of Crown Publishers.

ATF/ATA
Advanced Tactical Aircraft
by Erik Simonsen

The winners among seven major airframe manufacturers, competing for what may be the largest aircraft procurement contract of this century, the Advanced Tactical Fighter (ATF), were announced on October 31, 1986. One team, headed by Lockheed Aeronautical Systems Co. with General Dynamics and Boeing as partners, is building the YF-22A prototype. The YF-23A is being built by Northrop Corp. with McDonnell Douglas as principal subcontractor.

The final configurations of both prototypes have been frozen. Each is being hand-built in a race to be the best and, for psychological reasons, the first to fly. Each team will produce two flight vehicles so that two engine types can be flight tested on each prototype.

Pratt & Whitney and General Electric (GE) are producing the YF-119 and YF-120 powerplants, respectively. These advanced engines will feature technology far beyond the operational engines of today. High heat resistant ceramics in place of metal, fuel additives to reduce infrared (IR) signatures, increased thrust-to-weight ratios, and sustained supersonic cruise without afterburners are a few of the advances expected.

Both the YF-22A and YF-23A will be equipped with two-dimensional thrust vectoring/thrust reversing engine nozzles. This will give the ATF the required short-or-damaged runway capability as well as increased inflight maneuverability.

A McDonnell Douglas F-15 S/MTD (Short Takeoff and Landing/Maneuver Technology Demonstrator) has made its first flight at the St. Louis plant. It features forward canards derived from F/A-18 horizontal stabilizers. A two-dimensional nozzle system will be added to the aft section and, as flight testing begins, McDonnell Douglas will begin collecting data. The inflight characteristics of the system will provide valuable input for the YF-23A flight control software.

AGILE DEMONSTRATOR

Within the realm of thrust vectoring technology an entirely new aircraft, the X-31A, will be flying by late 1989. The X-31A EFM (Enhanced Fighter Maneuverability) is being built by Rockwell International and MBB of West Germany. The EFM program is sponsored by the Defense Advanced Research Projects Agency (DARPA), the Department of the Navy and the German Ministry of Defense (GMOD). The X-31A design will introduce three-dimensional thrust vectoring with paddle-like devices placed at 120-degree intervals around the tail cone. The action of the thrust vectoring paddles, close-coupled with the flight control system, will allow flight beyond the normal "stall-barrier." The unique approach will greatly increase close-in air combat maneuvering. This technology could prove extremely useful in the flight software and/or airframe design of future agile fighters.

The Air Force has established a series of stringent parameters to guide the design and demonstrator/validation phase of the ATF. Both teams hope to get their prototypes in the air in early 1990 and complete the demonstrator/validation phase by the end of the year. The contract is a big one with deliveries for the winner set to begin in 1993. The Air Force expects to order about 750 ATFs. This, however, could increase by several hundred if the Navy opts for the ATF as its fleet defense fighter of the late 1990s.

ATF MISSION REQUIREMENTS

Air superiority over the enemy's turf is the prime goal of the ATF. This requires long-legs at supersonic speeds and extended loiter capability in high-threat environments. It means sustained cruise at Mach 2 without afterburners and a Mach 3-plus dash capability. As if this were not enough, the Air Force wants the same airplane to be able to operate from limited or damaged runways and spring to a service ceiling of 85,000 feet and above. All of these capabilities must be packaged in an aircraft that has a maximum weight of 50,000 pounds and a unit fly-away cost of $35 million in 1985 dollars.

The ATF will have to operate in the central European combat environment. Sophisticated and highly integrated air defense systems, combined with lookdown/shootdown Su-27 Flanker, MiG-29 Fulcrum and other Soviet fighters

now under development, will be there to meet any approaching ATFs. According to early reports, however, it is believed the ATF will have such stealth capability that it will remain undetected by Soviet fighters until almost within visual range. That is, if the hostile fighters have survived the ATF's beyond visual range missile salvo. Besides having a new generation cannon on board, the ATF is expected to carry four SIDEWINDERs and four AMRAAMs (Advanced Medium Range Air-to-Air Missiles). The ATF will be able to track hostile targets at long range with onboard passive systems and E-3A AWACS datalink.

THE ATF TEAMS

Competition is expected to be intense during the YF-22A/YF-23A flyoff. Both teams are well equipped technologically to handle the design and production of the ATF. We may be reminded, in many ways, of the YF-16/YF-17 contest in the mid-1970s.

LOCKHEED/BOEING/
GENERAL DYNAMICS

The YF-22A ATF prototype being built by the Lockheed team will be aided by a wealth of corporate knowledge. Lockheed's unique experience with low observable aircraft dates back to the U-2, A-12, SR-71 and right up to the classified stealth systems of today. Existence of the F-117A 'Stealth Fighter' was announced by the Pentagon on November 10, 1988. Lockheed-built prototypes began flight testing during 1978 and the type became operational in 1983. A total of 59 of the sophisticated strike fighters are to be procured by the Air Force — joining a family of specialized stealth aircraft.

An unprecedented blend of technologies is being merged into the YF-22A design. The "pilot's associate" — a concept of an electronic copilot able to integrate all aspects of air-to-air combat, voice activated call-up of cockpit displays/functions, and weapons release — is now being designed and programmed at

Lockheed. Within the labs at Lockheed, "electric paint" has been developed. This material can conduct electricity and be applied to electronic circuitry or non-metallic aircraft structure and skin.

Boeing, now assembling the wings and aft section of the YF-22A, has extensive experience in airframe mass production, wing camber design (Mission Adaptive Wing-MAW) and lightweight composites. Boeing is also a major subcontractor on the B-2 ATB. Approximately 40 to 60 percent of the YF-22A will be constructed of graphite and thermo plastic composites.

The MAW, designed by Boeing and flown on the NASA F-111/AFTI aircraft, changed the wing camber to suit the flight envelope without the use of conventional slats or flaps. Boeing has established a firm data base to apply to ATF design parameters. A recent Boeing release on the MAW stated that it will provide optimum lift and reduced drag for any flight mode and automatically adjust in order to maintain the most efficient conditions. In addition, a fully adjustable camber will produce the same optimum results in all situations, including evasive action, tight turns, weapons delivery and efficient cruise.

F-16 TEST BEDS

General Dynamics has been flying a modified F-16/AFTI CCV (Control Configured Vehicle) since 1982 at Edwards Air Force Base (AFB), California. Resulting data have been impressive. The flight control system working in conjunction with the two canted canards beneath the fuselage allows for several new maneuvering techniques to be tested. Among the inflight maneuvers perfected were off bore-sight side-slip, climb and dive without nose pitch changes, controlled nose pitch without changing flight path, and flat turns without banking.

A new triplex fly-by-wire control system allowed for an automatic flight envelope fire control system for attack and egress. Several other systems, including an Automated Maneuver Attack System (AMAS) and a FLIR (Forward Looking Infra Red) pod were tested in both the air-to-air and air-to-ground mode. Advanced phases of cockpit voice command/control underwent extensive inflight testing and now data are being utilized in the ATF cockpit software. The Air Force has directed that, when possible, the cockpit and flight control software be integrated with the Agile Falcon being developed as an F-16C/D follow-on.

The F-16XL (F-16F) cranked-arrow delta design provided General Dynamics with an excellent test bed. The new composite wing contained 120 percent more area than the conventional F-16. With two 28-inch fuselage plugs and the new wing, the XL provided data for massive composite "wet wings," semi-conformal weapons and higher non-afterburning penetration speeds. The XL's range was 48 percent greater than the standard F-16 on internal fuel only and 87 percent greater with external tanks.

NORTHROP/ MCDONNELL DOUGLAS

A leading low observable technology developer, Northrop is currently producing the first six B-2 Advanced Technology Bomber (ATB) prototypes. The bomber is subsonic and totally dependent on Stealth and electronic warfare (EW) deception to achieve its mission goals. The B-2 is the largest Department of Defense (DoD) project ever to be totally designed by computer. The system utilizes a three-dimensional electronic database that can examine any part or piece of structure before fabrication begins. More information will become public as the B-2 eases from the black classification to the white.

The experience operating a "factory of the future" will certainly help in gearing up for ATF. Experience in making unstable and unusual shapes fly has allowed Northrop designers to move away from conventional fighter designs. It has been reported that Northrop has eliminated conventional horizontal and vertical stabilizers on the YF-23A design. To reduce RCS and aerodynamic drag, scaled down canted tailerons might appear on the YF-23A. A triple-redundant flight control system and continuous deflection-control on the tailerons will keep the inherently unstable design — stable. An unstable design is not a negative!

With it, one achieves agility.

McDonnell Douglas is a powerhouse partner to have in a heated contest. If the product is high-tech aircraft in mass production, the list is impressive — F-15D/E, F/A-18, AV-8B, T-45, C-17 and several civilian airliner types.

The F-15 S/MTD is now flying and the two-dimensional vectoring nozzle system will be installed in early 1989. Valuable flight data will be collected on the interaction of the flight controls with this system.

A great deal of research has been directed towards the ATF pilot and assets available to him. Both Northrop and McDonnell Douglas are investing heavily in simulation systems. Complete tactical scenarios with 150-degree, and soon to come, 360-degree field of view domes are being expanded at both company facilities.

Northrop's new Integration Simulation Systems Laboratory (ISSL) can present a complete three-dimensional air combat situation outside the cockpit and prioritize massive amounts of information for the pilot — inside the cockpit. In addition, the cockpit can be quickly reconfigured to aid engineers in the search for the optimum design.

General Dynamics F-16/AFTI CCV (above). Artist's concept of the ATF (opposite).

McDonnell Douglas currently is working on the Navy A-12 Advanced Tactical Aircraft (ATA). The medium-attack bomber will emphasize stealth technology and will become operational in the mid-1990s. This concurrent work will strengthen important areas within McDonnell Douglas.

NEW TECHNOLOGY FOR THE NAVY

Shadow, Ghost, Seabat, Avenger, Enforcer and Stingray are the leading contenders to name the Navy's newest attack aircraft — the A-12 Advanced Tactical Aircraft (ATA). This aircraft development program is highly classified. Few press reports, much less details, have emerged on its configuration.

On December 23, 1987, the Department of the Navy awarded McDonnell Douglas and General Dynamics a $241,000 contract to begin advanced engineering work on the ATA. This was followed in January 1988 with a $4.38 billion contract for full-scale development and production of the A-12. Production numbers could exceed 450 by several hundred if the Air Force opts for the ATA as an F/FB-111 and F-15E replacement during the late 1990s. The main purpose for the procurement of the A-12 is to replace the Grumman A-6E/G Intruder, which is the Navy's primary carrier based medium bomber. New technology is quickly needed in this area to increase survivability in high-threat arenas.

The Grumman A-6 Intruder series has been serving as an all-weather day/night stable weapons platform since 1958. It performed with precision during the Vietnam War and continues to be upgraded to meet current threats. Grumman is currently updating the A-6E to a "G" standard and was teamed with Northrop for the very pivotal ATA competition. The award to General Dynamics/McDonnell Douglas leaves Grumman, with the exception of the F-14D, temporarily out of future Navy aircraft production.

LADY IN BLACK

Several years ago, the increasing sophistication of our potential adversaries' air defense systems led the Navy to embark on an entirely new design for the medium bomber role. Thus, the cloaked ATA program was off and running. Due to the black classification status of the program, one can only speculate if a flyoff of prototype or scaled-down versions of such was held. The selection process could have been a computer/paper exercise because of recent advances.

Originally, the Navy wanted a single aircraft type to handle fleet defense and the attack-bomber role. However, as Stealth characteristics moved into the forefront of ATA design, this strategy was altered. Achieving optimum low observability requires aerodynamic tradeoffs. The fleet defense fighter role, now carried out by the F-14, requires supersonic dash and loiter capability as well as agility. These performance parameters and stealth design do not go hand in

(Above) The McDonnell Douglas F-15S/MTD (Short Takeoff Landing/Maneuver Technology Demonstrator).
(Left) Artist's concept of the Navy's newest attack aircraft-the A-12 Advanced Tactical Aircraft (ATA).

hand. Therefore, the A-12 will most likely be a subsonic aircraft powered by two GE F404 derivatives. A two-man crew will be flying an aircraft with entirely new state-of-the-art avionics and electronic warfare technology.

A COOPERATIVE EFFORT

To reduce overall future aircraft procurement costs, a Memorandum of Understanding (MoU) was signed by the Air Force and Navy during the spring of 1986. The MoU proposed a cooperative plan in which the Navy would study the USAF/ATF as an F-14D replacement. Likewise, the USAF would consider the A-12/ATA as a replacement for the F/FB-111 and F-15E in the late 1990s. The winning team could wind up producing several hundred navalized versions of the ATF to serve as a fleet defense fighter. Both ATF contenders have twin-engine designs with a weight limit set at 50,000 pounds.

The Navy would prefer a two-seater. Both ATF designs, however, are single-seaters.

The Air Force and Navy have had limited success in such cooperative efforts in the past. However, due to current fiscal constraints and Congressional pressure, more positive results could be forthcoming.

One interesting aspect of the ATA contract is that the first batch of A-12s will be developed jointly by the team of General Dynamics and McDonnell Douglas. From then on the contractors will split up and compete with each other on a yearly basis. The Navy will subsequently award the larger production lot to the lower bidder.

It will be very interesting to see which design course the Navy has chosen: a radical design based on recent advances in computer aided design and low observables, or a more conservative approach to minimize risk and possible cost overruns.

Whichever design was approved and is now being built, it will still be cloaked and out of view for some time. Even the ATF designs probably will not be revealed until taxi tests begin. For whatever shape we first see cutting through the skies, from the cockpit environment to the materials holding it together, the ATF and ATA will be technological leaps of vast importance. IDA

**Artist concept of the
Rockwell/MBB X-31A EFM.**

America continues its interplanetary search for knowledge about the universe. Charting paths beyond man's earlier grasp, we are moving ever farther into space. Imagination and technology have lifted its limits, allowing us to peer incredulously at an unknown world.

The United States space shuttle has opened new horizons in the stratosphere and represents only the beginning in the realm of space research. Shared by the National Space and Aeronautics Administration (NASA) and the Department of Defense (DoD), exploration projects are proving to be highly successful and significant. Yet to come are roles for military man-in-space ventures with the space station and the spaceplane.

Defense and aerospace activities are inseparable today. The new initiatives they spawn are rooted in man's earliest search for technology that allows him to soar skyward — higher and higher. We see the future in the dramatic efforts of the past, described in the following article on "Spaceplanes." And we know the defense of America and the Free World has moved into the space age.

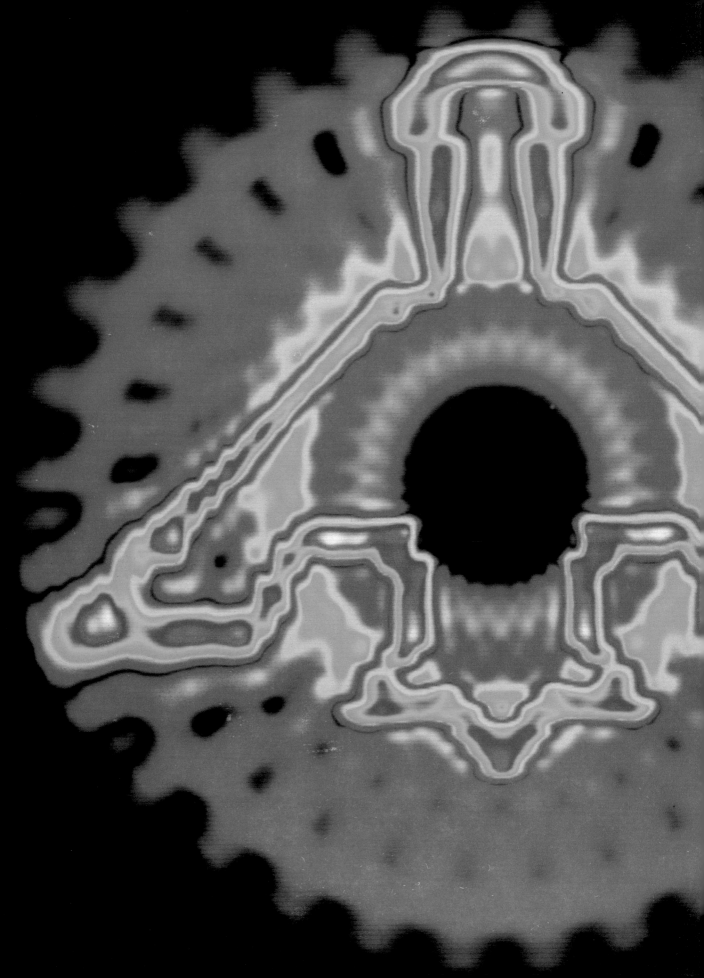

SPACEPLANES
Hypersonic Transport

by John Guthrie

T he structure of today's hypersonic research programs portends a new era in technology development. It is characterized by great expense, joint-financing, multi-agency and multi-national cooperation. We now live within a techno-logical era defined by the products of systems engineering. Tomorrow's technology products will go beyond systems engineering — to systems integration using computerized extrapolations of past knowledge to chart paths into the unknown.

The concepts for "Spaceplanes" have been at the vanguard of technological challenge since their inception in Russia in the 1860s. There, a small group of scientists, revolutionaries and technical enthusiasts achieved very real insights into the mechanics and principles of such things as reac-tion-control systems, vertical takeoff of winged vehicles and even trans-atmospheric and inter-atmospheric spaceflight using winged rockets! Some of their notions took 70 years to appear in the West.

The Russian pioneers of "Spaceplanes" struggled under the most dire social and scientific condi-tions. Their work was individually financed. None-theless, they charted the principles of interplane-tary flight, using just their brains, some writing in-struments and Newtonian physics. Their research methodology has defined the 20th Century Soviet tradition of theoretical scientific advancement.

This computer-enhanced photo shows a reconstruction of a drawing resembling a delta-wing aircraft, using a set of fundamental image components. The components are being used at Sandia National Laboratories in Livermore, Calif., to design a new kind of optical holo-graphic filter. The "lock-and-tumbler" hologram will be used in an optical pattern recognition system to recognize objects regardless of their location or angle of view.

The second developmental phase of "Spaceplanes" started in Germany during the 1930s. The military recognized the advantages to be gained by developing "ultra" technologies that lay beyond legal precedent. The Versailles Treaty, imposed on the nation after World War I, prohibited German development of bomber aircraft, but said nothing about ballistic missiles or hypersonic "Spaceplanes." Thus, the Germans culled from Russia, America and Europe the technology, doctrine, hardware, and software of hypersonic flight. Hypersonics refers to atmospheric flight at over five times the speed of sound. Here the extreme temperatures and elevated pressures caused by the passing of an object through air causes chemical and shockwave interactions that are noticeably different from those encountered at supersonic flight speeds. The predominant challenge in early hypersonic research was not propulsion but in solving the "reentry problem" which severely limited the military utility of ballistic missiles.

As ballistic missile technology improved in the 1950s, the first plans for an American hypersonic bomber and covert military reconnaissance/surveillance vehicles were based on rocket-powered boost-gliders, using skip-glide reentry techniques to absorb the heat load of reentry and then "bouncing" back into space, temporarily, to shed the heat by radiation.

Such semi-ballistic "Spaceplanes" were already obsolete because of the rapid improvement of ground-to-air/space defensive missiles. Economically, spy satellites were a more cost-effective technology alternative. In terms of arms control and verification, silo-based ICBM's were "stabilizing." Manned hypersonic systems were considered destabilizing because one could not know for sure if such a vehicle was on a photo mission or a bomb run. This was the effect of systems engineering, the third phase of "Spaceplane" technology development. Systems that looked great on paper just didn't perform, or were dangerous to the real world. Many consider SDI/"Star Wars" to be such a proposal.

The first hypersonic object was a ballistic missile payload that flew in 1949. Soon thereafter, plans were devised for the first winged hypersonic test vehicle, the manned X-15. It became the ultimate aeronautical research program of the 1950s. The X-15 was seen as "Round Two" of the very successful "X-plane" flight research experiments, Round One being the series of supersonic test flights of the X-1, X-2 and unmanned X-7 ramjet testbed, etc.. From 1961-1968, the X-15 test program included 199 flights, including excursions past 350,000 feet altitudes and speeds to Mach 6.7.

Like the ballistic missiles and hypersonic atmospheric sounding rockets that preceded it, the X-15

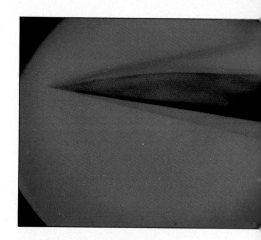

was rocket-powered. Jet engine development had reached an apparent zenith with the ramjets flown on the X-7. These ramjets used inlet spike geometry to "capture" the incoming supersonic flow, slowing it through the engine's combustor to subsonic speeds. The conventional wisdom was that jet engines could only operate with subsonic combustion. This limited their performance to supersonic speeds in the Mach 4 range.

It was left to Fred Billig, a graduate student at Johns Hopkins Applied Physics Lab, in 1957, to prove that combustion could exist in supersonic flows and that the flame wouldn't be "blown out." Billig's research led to a patent application in 1958 (classified until 1981) for what has come to be known as the supersonic combustion ramjet. The term "scramjet" was first used by Billig in describing a Supersonic Combustion Ramjet Missile he was working on for the U.S. Navy and by Marequardt in California in their description of engines under development. Between 1965 and 1968, a number of scramjet engines produced net positive thrust. Topping the list was Billig's missile scramjet which created 11 Gs of axial acceleration at Mach 5 using highly-reactive chemical fuels. This engine was later tested to Mach 7.2. Scramjets offered rocket-like performances, using the much more efficient method of jet propulsion — utilizing the atmospheric oxygen to support combustion, not a heavy tankful of on-board oxidizer.

Starting in the late 1950s, the USAF began looking at aerospace systems offering greater operational flexibility than the earlier technology

The Sanger-Bredt Antipodal Bomber, designed during WWII, as a rocket-propelled boost-glider, utilizing "skip-glide" reentry technique. American military planners recognized that the hypersonic speed of such a vehicle made it an attractive delivery system for nuclear warheads.

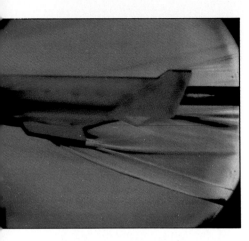

NASA wind tunnel test from 1974 shows the shockwave interactions that typify Airframe-Integrated Scramjets. In a Mach 6 flow, this model's nose acts as an aerospike, defining the hypersonic shockwave so that along the fuselage forebody a stable flow can be captured by the scramjet combustor, which extends into the flow. After combustion, the scramjet exhaust expands against the fuselage afterbody, creating lift.

could provide. A hybrid form of rocket propulsion called the Liquid Air Cycle Engine (LACE) was seen as a way of achieving Single-Stage-to-Orbit (SSTO). The vehicle concept under study was called the Aerospaceplane. As it flew, the LACE engine would scoop up air and chill this airflow using the on-board liquid hydrogen fuel, until the air liquified. Then the fuel and liquified oxidizer would be burned in the LACE rocket chamber. The idea was good, but the efficiencies were low, due largely to the weight of massive heat-exchangers.

Growing out of Aerospaceplane came a scramjet concept from NASA and the Garrett company called the Hypersonic Research Engine (HRE). It was a research program having as its ultimate goal the flight test of a working scramjet on the X-15. In 1967, ground testing of structural strength and aerothermal (heat flow) characteristics led up to the flight testing of an HRE "shape" — a dummy scramjet — on the ventral fin of the X-15.

Following a preliminary stability and control flight with the HRE to Mach 4.7, an all-out X-15 flight took place that set the unofficial world speed record at Mach 6.7. During the latter flight, the HRE dummy was entirely burned off the ventral fin by the intense shockwave interactions between fin, engine pod and fuselage.

The HRE testing showed that podded, axisymetric scramjets were problematic in hypersonic applications, due to the lack of integration with airframes. The experience gained in the HRE program gave NASA (Langley Research Center,

Virginia in particular) impetus to continue testing on their own, even after the USAF abandoned scramjets in the 1970s. Following the HRE experiments, in 1968, NASA Langley continued scramjet research with the Airframe-Integrated Scramjet (AIS) program. By 1973, NASA had settled on an AIS design that utilized the fuselage forebody as the air compression surface. The scramjet itself then acts only as a combustor, and the fuselage afterbody substitutes for a jet-expansion nozzle. Thus powered, the hypersonic vehicle rides on the lift created by shockwave interactions. This is the mode of scramjet propulsion fundamental to all of the contemporary work underway. Following the completion of the X-15 program, a few hypersonic flight test programs were proposed, but none were funded. A "Round

Three" approach to the X-planes was considered in the form of a manned boost-glider called the X-20 DYNA-SOAR. The X-20 was proposed in conjunction with a military space station called the Manned Orbiting Lab (MOL). In 1976, a joint (DoD/NASA) National Hypersonic Flight Research Facility (NHFRF) was suggested. It would have combined a number of facilities and research capabilities into one overall program, but funding was not forthcoming.

Compared to the rapid technologic strides made in the 1950s, the field of scramjet propulsion and hypersonic aerodynamics was virtually abandoned during the 1970s. America did get a "Spaceplane," but it came from the "other side of the house", the one that brought the country ICBMs, Mercury, Gemini and Apollo.

Named after the father of modern "Spaceplanes", the MBB Sanger II is conceived as having a manned, ramjet-powered first stage, roughly the size of a Boeing 747 (80 meter length X 50 meter span) and weighing 410,000 kg. The six ramjets will, according to the flight profile defined by MBB, take the second stage orbiter to 114,000 ft and Mach 7 before staging. The rocket-powered orbiter will be about 27m long, with a 12m span and will weigh about 90,000 kg, fully loaded.

An unmanned Hypersonic Glide Vehicle (HGV) concept by Martin Marietta is one of the potential weapon systems which will benefit from the refined hypersonic data obtained by the NASA/X-30 program. The HGV concept calls for launch by ICBM along a depressed, endo-atmospheric trajectory that would permit the strike wepon to penetrate severe Soviet anti-missile defenses (ones programmed for ballistic threats like contemporary ICBM reentry vehicles).

With billions invested in vertical launch facilities, the United States Government went ahead with a modified, stripped-down version of the Space Transportation System (STS). Scott Crossfield, the first X-15 test pilot, referred to the Shuttle as something akin to a 1930s-era aluminum glider, "crammed with computers to make it fly and covered with bricks to keep it from burning up."

Plans for the U.S. Space Shuttle were tied — not coincidentally — to plans for a U.S. Space Station. These joint concepts, first described in Russia nearly a hundred years earlier, have also been adopted by the USSR.

Even before the U.S. Shuttle flew in 1981, the shortcomings of the STS were apparent to the U.S. military. Within the USAF Systems Command and Space Command, attention was given to the future military requirements of assured-access to both air and space environments. An emerging doctrine of trans-atmospheric warfare soon evolved, along with contractor proposals for rocket-powered vehicles, since scramjet efficiencies were still too low. The U.S. Air Force Manned Aerospace Vehicles and Trans-atmospheric Vehicles (MAVs and TAVs) were variously capable of inter-orbital plane changes.

The breakthrough in scramjet propulsion occurred during the early 1980s and culminated in mid-1985, during a classified technology survey program that was conducted by the Defense Advanced Research Projects Agency (DARPA). This survey,

code named COPPER CANYON, identified the breakthroughs in hypersonic propulsion, aircraft materials and structures, computational fluid dynamics and flight control that could enable air-breathing SSTO. It was out of COPPER CANYON that the program known today as National Aero-Space Plane (NASP) was created. As was the case with the proposed NHFRF that preceded it in the 1970s, the NASP program is a research collective, formed from various U.S. military and civilian agencies and their facilities. The five-agency NASP partnership (NASA, DARPA, USAF, Navy and SDIO) is working to create a single capability: air-breathing SSTO.

NASP research is now in the development phase of creating the required "enabling technologies" to achieve SSTO. In 1994, the researchers hope to proceed with the flight test of an SSTO vehicle that has been dubbed the X-30. This flight research vehicle will probably be about the size of a commercial DC-9, but weighing only about as much as an F-15. One engineer has described the proposed X-30 as resembling a "fat B-1B," with the predominant structure being a large liquid hydrogen tank. The NASP is requiring an unprecedented degree of cooperation between three airframe contractors: McDonnell Douglas, Rockwell and General Dynamics; and the two principal propulsion contractors, Pratt & Whitney and Rocketdyne. This is because of the complex interactions that exist between hypersonic airframes and engines.

Modeling these interactions is the job of supercomputers. Half of the supercomputers in the U.S. are doing NASP-related computations and the hypersonic program may stimulate faster machines sooner than expected. Computational codes alone can predict the behavior of gasses and body shapes beyond the Mach 8 limit of "real gas" ground test facilities. The output of experimental codes is being compared to wind tunnel test data on subscale models and against the flight test experience of vehicles like the X-15, Shuttle and classified military reentry test shapes.

As the SSTO vehicle burns a hole in the sky at Mach 25, the gasses passing through the scramjet will be combusting at speeds of only about Mach 8 (the lower Mach is caused by heating of the gas). Even so, the "residence time" of hydrogen fuel in a two-foot long scramjet combustor is only on the order of tenths of milliseconds. The engine components, like the airframe's, must be fabricated from metallic thermal protection materials that can be formed into complex aerodynamic geometries. This requirement — and the problems inherent in Shuttle-type tiles — has moved the NASP in the direction of some of the most exotic metallurgy in the world.

Powder metallurgy "locks in" the best high temperature strength properties of titanium, while preserving the metal's malleability. It can be pressed into complex shapes that previously would have destroyed titanium. Oxide-inhibiting coatings are being developed, so that the metals don't vaporize in the highly-energized flow of passing atmospheric molecules. A new class of "intermetallics" (bimetallic alloys with highly-ordered crystal structures) has been developed which offers extreme strength at temperatures near 1,700-1,800 degrees Fahrenheit (F). A NASP vehicle must endure such temperatures on panels near leading edges. The nosecap of a NASP-class vehicle will probably be made of reinforced carbon-carbon, capable of withstanding temperatures of nearly 3,000 degrees F. Special anti-oxidation agents are being developed for nosecaps and leading edges.

This is the "hat trick" of air-breathing SSTO — the supercold hydrogen fuel will be routed from the NASP fuel tank and circulated through the airframe and engine, prior to burning, absorbing as much heat as possible from the vehicle and converting this into additional energy for combustion. Can enough heat be transferred into the combustor to accelerate to Mach 26 at 150,000 feet, for example, in order for the vehicle to fall into space (and Mach 25 orbital velocity) under the force of its momentum? Between now and 1993, that question should be answered, and the decision to proceed with the X-30 can be made.

Regardless of whether the NASP/ X-30 attains SSTO, or is even built, the NASP program will have a variety of useful military and commercial benefits for the U.S. Future unmanned military reconnaissance/ strike systems like the proposed USAF Hypersonic Glide Vehicle (HGV) will incorporate materials, structures and avionics that will be advanced by the NASP program. Likewise, the advances in computational fluid dynamics and materials will lead to more efficient and powerful military propulsion — supersonic and hypersonic.

Currently, the NASP contractor funding is virtually on-par with U.S. Government funding levels. Therefore, it is obvious that the private sector expects NASP to spawn a variety of highly-advanced applications, many of them commercial.

NASP / X-30 concept from General Dynamics.

Hypersonic research will enable new classes of endo-atmospheric supersonic and hypersonic transports to be financed and developed with greater assurance of the actual technical and economic risks involved. SSTO vehicles to service Low Earth Orbit facilities may actually be possible, opening up the age of space industry with launch costs one-tenth those of today's rocket systems. A range of other commercial "spinoffs" will be certain, leading to lighter, stronger materials, more efficient fuel management, hydrogen fuel usage and highly-capable computers.

The success of hypersonic research during the next decade — whether the technology goals themselves are attained or not — may well be best measured in terms relating to the participants themselves. For the pursuit of hypersonics is creating a new hypersonic culture, drawing out the best of the military, science and industry.

What lies ahead can easily stretch one's imagination. The future is the realm of hypersonic research, which will build on the ideas that have been envisioned over the years. The age of "Spaceplanes" may well be at hand. IDA

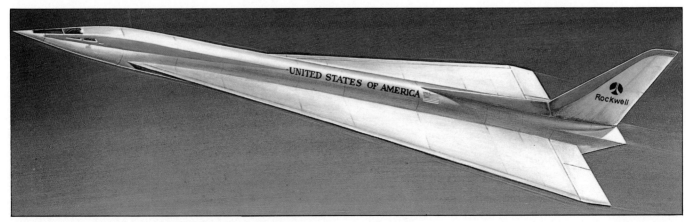

NASP / X-30 concept from Rockwell International.

AMERICA'S

USS CONSTELLATION Air Wing Flyby

BEST

Northrop F-5 Tiger II

(top to bottom) McDonnell Douglas F-15 Eagle,
F-4 Phantom, FA-18, and General Dynamics F-16 Falcon

U.S. Navy F-21 Kfir, manufactured by IAI